THE ONE-MINUTE MEETING

THE ONE-MINUTE MEETING

Creating Student Stakeholders in Schools

Mary Hemphill, Ph.D.

cognella®
SAN DIEGO

Bassim Hamadeh, CEO and Publisher
Jennifer McCarthy, Field Acquisitions Editor
Amy Smith, Senior Project Editor
Casey Hands, Production Editor
Emely Villavicencio, Senior Graphic Designer
Stephanie Kohl, Licensing Coordinator
Natalie Piccotti, Director of Marketing
Kassie Graves, Vice President of Editorial
Jamie Giganti, Director of Academic Publishing

Cover image: Copyright © 2019 iStockphoto LP/discan.
Copyright © 2019 iStockphoto LP/Big_and_serious.

Design Image: Copyright © 2014 Depositphotos/orelphoto2.
Design Image: Copyright © 2013 Depositphotos/Glopphy.
Design Image: Copyright © 2020 Depositphotos/PainterMaster.

Printed in the United States of America.

cognella® | ACADEMIC PUBLISHING
3970 Sorrento Valley Blvd., Ste. 500, San Diego, CA 92121

ACTIVE LEARNING

For readers or educators looking to complement the reading, this book has videos and interactive activities available through Cognella Active Learning. To access the digital content, go to https://active.cognella.com/courses/4643.

This book is dedicated to my mother, who showed me the power of words from the moment I entered the world and helped me cultivate that power throughout my journey.

BRIEF CONTENTS

PREFACE   XV

PART 1   The School   1

Chapter 1   Every School Has a Story   2

Chapter 2   The Needs Assessment   11

Chapter 3   The Mission Statement   22

PART 2   The Students   31

Chapter 4   Students as Stakeholders   32

Chapter 5   Students as Evaluators   42

Chapter 6   Students as Change Agents   50

PART 3   The Questions   59

Chapter 7   How Are You Doing Today?   60

Chapter 8   What Is Your Greatest Celebration or
What Are You Most Proud of From the
Past 9 Weeks (Quarter/Semester)?   69

Chapter 9   What Challenges or Concerns Are You Experiencing in Your Class(es) or in Our School?   78

PART 4   The Strategy   89

Chapter 10   Mobilizing the Instructional Leadership Team   90

Chapter 11   Communicating With Teacher Leaders   99

Chapter 12   Preparing the Mobile Office   109

PART 5   The Data   121

Chapter 13   Identifying Trends and Themes   122

Chapter 14   Implementing and Sustaining Change   132

Chapter 15   Balancing Transformation and Testing   139

REFERENCES   147

INDEX   151

DETAILED CONTENTS

Preface   xv

PART I   The School   1

CHAPTER 1

Every School Has a Story   2

What Does It Mean to Dream?   4
The School Report Card   6
The Walmart© Conversation   7

CHAPTER 2

The Needs Assessment   11

Informal Data Versus Formal Data   12
Identifying 3-Year Trends   13
Content Area Data   14
Behavioral Data   14
Every Behavior Communicates Something   15
    Major Versus Minor Behaviors   15
Location, Location, Location   16
Measuring Mental Health   17
Physical Data   17
Shifting Perspective   18
Conducting a Facility Walk-Through   19

CHAPTER 3

The Mission Statement   22

Can Anyone Recite the Mission Statement?   24
Developing the Mission   25
Marketing the Mission   28

PART 2   The Students   31

CHAPTER 4

Students as Stakeholders   32

Abandoning the Top-Down Approach   34
The One-Minute Meeting Conceptual Framework   36
    Transformational Leadership   36
    Student Stakeholders   36
    Shared Vision   37
    Schools as Learning Communities   38
The 21st Century Is Here   39

CHAPTER 5

Students as Evaluators   42

Creating Opportunities for Feedback   44
Teaching Evaluative Language to Students   45
Student Surveys   47

CHAPTER 6

Students as Change Agents   50

Addressing the Leadership Gap   52
An Attitude of Excellence   53
A Culture of High Expectations   55

PART 3   The Questions   59

CHAPTER 7

How Are You Doing Today?   60

Rita F. Pierson—Every Kid Needs a Champion   62
Implementing Question #1   64
How Are You Doing Today? More Than an Icebreaker   66

CHAPTER 8

What Is Your Greatest Celebration or What Are
You Most Proud of From the Past 9 Weeks
(Quarter/Semester)?   69

Every Student Has a Celebration   71
Implementing Question #2   72
"I Don't Know" Is Not an Option   76

CHAPTER 9

What Challenges or Concerns Are You Experiencing in Your Class(es) or in Our School?   78

Bloom Versus Maslow   80
Implementing Question #3   81
Hearing Ears and Walking Feet   85

PART 4   The Strategy   89

CHAPTER 10

Mobilizing the Instructional Leadership Team   90

Connecting the Mission Statement   92
Practice Makes Pragmatic   93
Scheduling the School Leader   95
Scheduling Tips for the School Leader   96

CHAPTER 11

Communicating With Teacher Leaders   99

True School Improvement From the Inside Out   101
More Than a Memo   103
    Sample One-Minute Meeting Memo   105
From Automatic to Autonomy   106

CHAPTER 12

Preparing the Mobile Office   109

The Basics   111
Reflection Questions for Preparing the One-Minute Meeting
Mobile Office   111
Data Collection Tools and Templates   112
Technology   118

PART 5   The Data   121

CHAPTER 13

Identifying Trends and Themes   122

The Emotional Compass   124
Disaggregating and Analyzing the Responses   126

CHAPTER 14

Implementing and Sustaining Change   132

SITs and ILTs   134
Individual Teacher Leaders   136
Parents/Guardians, and Community Stakeholders   137

CHAPTER 15

Balancing Transformation and Testing   139

It Is a Process   142
Productive Failure   143
It's All About the People   145

References   147

Index   151

PREFACE

The One-Minute Meeting is an instructional practice that authentically involves students as primary stakeholders in their learning journey. In 60 seconds, school stakeholders can glean important information from students that helps to inform instructional practice, learning environment, and student achievement in their learning communities! The One-Minute Meeting creates a critical opportunity for school leaders, instructional lead teams, teacher leaders, and support staff to extend the space and purpose for student stakeholders to pull a seat up to the table and offer valuable insight and feedback on teaching and learning as it relates to their personal experience in school. This instructional practice captures students' multifaceted and multidimensional experiences and then uses those findings to further inform the pedagogy, practice, and processes in the learning environment from the unique perspective of our most important client: the students!

The One-Minute Meeting was birthed from one school leader's need to transform a low-performing school into a school of excellence for a demographic of high-poverty learners. I was honored to serve as the proud principal of what was once deemed a "low-performing" school by the state of North Carolina. In our team's efforts to provide our students with a quality, 21st-century learning experience, our teacher leaders, community stakeholders, and school and district leaders joined us on the journey of thinking outside the crayon box to effect positive change at Fannie Tyson (FT) Elementary. As our Instructional Lead Team began to tackle the colossal task of identifying key stakeholders in the transformational process, our students were identified as the VIPs in our needs assessment. To fully understand the depth and breadth of the key changes we were making to instructional programs, implementation, pedagogy, instructional resources, culture, and climate, we needed their perspective and feedback to undergird these changes and add validity to the transformational processes. In a conversation with our Instructional Lead Team weeks before we started the first round of One-Minute Meetings at FT Elementary, I stated, "There are a lot of things we do in schools that feel good and make sense to adults, but how do we know what students think about this work?" Two weeks later, the first communication went out to teachers about the One-Minute Meeting, describing the process in detail. Since that first round, the One-Minute Meetings became a cornerstone of our quarterly data dives, and we used the information shared by our students to continually evolve and inform our practice at our school.

This book takes the reader on an in-depth journey through the need for student stakeholders to sit at the table as vocal and viable participants in shared educational decision making. Following a chapter format with actual narratives and testimonials, this book will lay out in detail how to introduce, plan, implement, and disaggregate the One-Minute Meeting from start to finish in any learning environment. With in-depth explanations on the importance of each One-Minute Meeting component, this text is an easy, yet intriguing, read that purposes to inspire school and district leaders to engage fully with their learners on a level that empowers students to have a voice in the learning process. Each chapter begins with a narrative that explains the birth of a key One-Minute Meeting concept and then lays out the formal research supporting that concept in a school setting. Close attention has been given to the parallels between low performance, Title I, and/or schools that cater to populations with high free and reduced lunch and empowering students and teacher leaders. In addition, the text provides exemplars and templates within various chapters that support implementation at the elementary, middle, and high school levels.

This book presents each component of the One-Minute Meeting, including:

- identifying the purpose of the key component and introducing the concept;

- planning and organizing the needs assessment for pre-implementation of the One-Minute Meeting;

- emphasizing the importance and rationale of the three One-Minute Meeting questions;

- developing the mobile office;

- communicating with school stakeholders as shared decision makers and professional experts;

- capturing and disaggregating the data, as well as communicating findings to school stakeholders; and

- explaining the implications for future educational practice.

The book concludes with the impact that this innovative instructional practice has on the long-standing culture of standardized testing and the rapidly evolving need for problem solvers and solution seekers in our world today. At the end of each chapter, the reader will find a One-Minute Challenge that will help her/him to extend the content from the chapter into an actionable activity within the learning community. This challenge is designed specifically to be a brief, yet powerful bridge to transformation using One-Minute Meeting principles.

Lastly, a One-Minute Post-Pandemic Strategy has also been added to punctuate each chapter. As a global society, we will shift from the "new normal" to the "now normal" particularly in the educational arena. COVID-19 has forever revolutionized the way in which people, tech, time, space, and resources are utilized. Schools and districts will be tasked with redefining engagement, teaching, and learning for what will arguably be the next five to ten school years based on the impact of COVID-19, and the One-Minute Post-Pandemic strategy helps school leaders shift their approach when it comes to re-engaging student leaders in that effort.

I would like to acknowledge the supportive and inspirational team at Cognella Academic Publishing for their dedication to this project from start to finish, as well as to the team of reviewers who provided such thought-provoking and critical feedback:

Alecia Blackwood, University of Central Florida

Jess Gregory, Southern Connecticut State University

Joy Lewis, Daytona State College

Lavetta Henderson, Florida A&M University

Martha Wall-Whitfield, University of Arkansas—Little Rock

Suzanne Hardie, University of South Carolina

I want to acknowledge the students, teacher leaders, Instructional Lead Team, school support staff, district leaders, and community stakeholders who poured into FT Elementary during its transformation. Thank you for bringing your best selves into our learning community, thank you for allowing me to lead alongside you, and thank you for sharing your journey with us all. We are ready to learn, lead, and leverage much-needed change for students and schools everywhere.

PART 1

THE SCHOOL

Every School Has a Story

One-Minute Reflection Question:
How do we, as school leaders, begin the process of true school transformation as we encounter wounded stakeholders in broken schools?

In this chapter, school leaders will gain a first glimpse at a school through the eyes of a transformational school leader. To critically evaluate any school as a key stakeholder in the One-Minute Meeting process, the school leader must gain insight into the past and present environmental factors that have shaped its thinking, including physical features and conditions, instructional frameworks, behavioral concerns, communal perspectives and influences, and socioemotional impacts. Every school has a unique story with its own characters, settings, plot twists, and conflict. As the school's leader, one must willingly discover and masterfully navigate each school's narrative to begin writing a new chapter. This is one school's story.

Our students do not know how to dream.
—A passionate, but promising, teacher leader

As we rounded the corner and pulled onto the street leading toward my newest assignment, I lowered the window so that I could get a better look at the neighborhood surrounding the school. Before we had crossed the railroad tracks, the manicured lawns and perfectly spaced out historical houses welcomed everyone into this little town. Even the central office from which we had just departed was an old converted Belk building nestled squarely in the middle of downtown amid locally owned clothing stores, government structures, and the best neighborhood mechanic in town. Now having crossed over the railroad tracks, I could clearly see the dilapidated construction overgrown with kudzu and the tightly spaced single-family homes with multiple cars in the driveways, and on every corner sat a community church with welcome signs of faith and hope. The car began to slow down, and I realized that we must be near the school. After the school board meeting the night before, the five principals who had been named to schools in the district were informed that they would meet their new school families the following morning. I was fortunate to be escorted by the district's assistant superintendent of curriculum and instruction, along with the director of elementary education, and when the car came to a stop, I was the last to unbuckle my seat belt and exit the vehicle. The marquee at Fannie Tyson (FT) Elementary read *"EOGs are here. Make sure you study hard!"* And the lone sign near the front door reminded parents and guardians to sign their students up for Boy Scouts. This would be the first and last time I entered through the front doors of FT Elementary as a stranger because as I entered the school, I was home.

FT Elementary was a suburban school that served almost 415 students in grades pre-K through fifth grade. With almost 68% African American, 20% Caucasian, 10% Native American, and 2% other, this Title I school is steeped in tradition and historical context. Named for one of the late educational pioneers and social rights activists, over the past 60 years, the school has served the local community as a segregated high school, an integrated Academically Intellectually Gifted (AIG) magnet middle school, and now as a public elementary school. A picture of Fannie Tyson hung proudly in the foyer of the school, welcoming every student, parent, guardian, and visitor as a proverbial tipping of the hat to the past and a proverbial nod to the ever-changing and hopeful future. FT Elementary was proud to be a community school that partnered closely with area organizations, including the sororities and fraternities, local family-owned businesses, neighborhood churches, and nonprofits. With such a widespread and active alumni association, FT Elementary was fortunate to have stakeholders represented in every area from local health care, private business, community activism, and even law enforcement.

The school's vision statement embodied the characteristics of the school's mascot, the Jets, stating, "Each student soaring above and beyond to reach his or her fullest potential in a globally competitive society." To SOAR at FT Elementary meant that everyone in the building from the youngest 3-year-old to the most veteran staff member would practice self-control (S), organization (O), attentiveness (A), and responsibility (R) on a daily basis. Each morning, students and faculty would recite this pledge to SOAR during the morning announcement and the school's Positive Behavior Interventions & Supports (PBIS) program centered on those tenets. Unfortunately, with over 400 discipline referrals the year prior and with a lack of direction and leadership in the school's PBIS planning committee, FT Elementary failed to be recognized as a PBIS school for the past 2 years and the effects were far-reaching in the school community.

Newly released end-of-grade (EOG) scores and Education Value-Added Assessment System (EVAAS) data noted that in the 2014–2015 school year, FT Elementary did not meet growth on the school accountability growth estimates overall by –2.19. Student proficiency in the areas of reading and math were also dismal, with only 22% showing proficiency, respectively. In terms of educator effectiveness, FT Elementary also did not meet growth by –4.83. According to the state department of education, educator effectiveness is measured by the state's evaluation system and other informal means. The particular system utilized engages teachers, principals, and their evaluators in constructive conversation that recognizes educators' individual strengths and focuses on how they can improve their professional practice. Not only were students underachieving but also teacher leaders' productivity and success at FT Elementary dropped to an all-time low.

What Does It Mean to Dream?

To begin the work of transformation in any organization, particularly a struggling school, it is critical that the school leader takes the time to connect with and get to know the people who learn and lead within the learning community itself. Without a solid understanding of and appreciation for the people and where they came from, it is nearly impossible to envision a plan to determine where they are going. According to Dr. Neil Raisman (2012) in his blog post entitled "Students and Staff Are the Most Important Stakeholders and Customers on Campus,"

> Think of staff as the waiters and waitresses at the college as a restaurant. Staff are the ones who provide the table-side service to our customers, all of them by the way. If you don't treat them well or treat them rudely, your food will be served more slowly for example. Service will be slow and not very good so your entire meal experience will be lessened.

Educational research has long ignored the power of teacher leadership in public education; however, recent surges in academic literature are shifting from a focus on top-down leadership to a learning community model that embodies and empowers all stakeholders in the community as critical to the success of its students. Neumann, Jones, and Webb (2012) argue, "It is vital to disrupt the discourse that promotes the idea that principals or those outside the teaching profession as the definers of instructional knowledge" (p. 3). Teacher leadership speaks not only to the essence of developing and carrying out a shared vision within a school but also promotes teachers as critical players in the development of thriving learning communities. Day et al. (2003) offered insight on the four dimensions of teacher leadership as (1) strengthening of classroom practice, (2) encouraging teacher ownership in the change process, (3) assuming the mantle of teacher expert, and (4) engaging in collegiality for mutual learning. Teacher leaders are the quintessential definition of grassroots transformation in a struggling school because of their close proximity to and intense interaction with a school's most important customer: its students. School leaders who prioritize their efforts to support and develop teacher leadership within the building will reap dividends in the end.

When I first arrived at FT Elementary, I communicated with the school's faculty and staff regarding my desire to sit down with each of them individually, in pairs, or in grade-level teams to get to know them and begin discussing our strategy for forging into the new school year. My initial e-mail read as follows:

Greetings FT Elementary Family!

I hope that everyone was able to enjoy a wonderful and restful weekend. Although Wednesday is my first official day at FT Elementary, I wanted to take an opportunity to reach out to you and let you know how excited and honored I am to work with each of you. Education is probably the single-most important tool that our children, and we as adults, have in the 21st century. Education empowers minds to create new ideas, empowers individuals to be change agents, and empowers organizations to be influential resources for communities. The single-most extraordinary aspect of our profession is undoubtedly the people. From our littlest pre-K people to our veteran teachers and support staff, it is the people who make each day in public education unique, exciting, and interesting. If we respect and value each person who walks in this building during the 2015–2016 school year, we are going to make huge strides toward success!

In order to begin our journey, I would like to schedule time to sit down and meet with each of you individually or as grade-level teams (whichever is more comfortable). This includes meeting with teacher assistants, support staff, and cafeteria and custodial staff. My goal for these meetings is for us to gain some insight about each other as educators, as teammates, and as people in general. I would like you to come armed with any questions you have for the upcoming school year, celebrations you would like to share from the past school year, opportunities for improvement and insight on how to make FT Elementary the best place to learn and work in this district. Each person on this campus is critical to our success because the work we do for children can change their lives!

Please choose from the dates and time slots below. Simply respond to this e-mail with the date and time you wish and indicate if you are meeting with me individually or as a grade-level group. If none of the dates/times work with your schedule, please e-mail me and let me know when would work best for you, and we will work together to arrange an alternate meeting time.

Again, I appreciate your willingness to meet with me prior to the start of a new school year. The work that you do is invaluable, and I want to make sure that we start the 2015–2016 school year on a great note! I look forward to hearing from everyone soon and THANK YOU for all that you do! (:

Mary Hemphill, PhD
Principal
FT Elementary

Over the course of 3 weeks, I sat down with each and every faculty and staff member, as well as all the support staff, custodial, and cafeteria teams—54 meetings total! The FT family and I were able to begin paving their path to greatness by developing a relationship around their experiences! They shared with me their journeys prior to arriving at FT Elementary, celebrated their stories in and outside the FT classrooms, and discussed what we could do together to make FT Elementary the best place to work and learn in our school district. I captured each individual's responses on a legal pad, with their permission, and communicated to them that the information gleaned from our meeting would only be shared with the administration. During one particular conversation, I asked a teacher who was new to our building to tell me how we could transform FT Elementary into a school of excellence. She responded, "Well first, our students do not know how to dream. If they do not have a dream for themselves, then we have to dream for them. We have to teach them how to dream." That moment resonated at the forefront of our work at FT Elementary each day. I realized the significance of that encounter instantly. I had inherited a school full of wounded stakeholders: teachers and support staff who held the best interests of students in the palms of their beaten and bruised hands with only glimmers of hope shimmering underneath clouds of frustration, fatigue, and fear. Dreaming was not going to be measured on the EOG tests at the end of the school year, yet, somehow, we had to find a way to infuse dreaming into the curriculum immediately.

From those conversations, professional relationships birthed strategies that ultimately teachers would model in the classrooms. Each voice was heard when decisions were made by our instructional lead team (ILT) that summer, and I shared the responses from those intimate conversations in the utmost confidence with the leaders around the table. Each of our teachers' stories was etched into the future of our students' school year, and as we developed the vision and goals for the year ahead, we made sure that both of them were framed with dream dust.

The School Report Card

The state education department released the school report cards for the first time at the end of the 2012–2013 school year. In an effort to provide an informational resource to parents, educators, state leaders, researchers, and stakeholders about the state's public, charter, and alternative schools, the school report cards include general school information, overall student performance and characteristics, career and technical education (CTE) credentials, American College Testing (ACT) performance, teacher qualifications, and school environment demographics. According to state's education department, the school report cards help to provide transparency regarding the state's public schools, particularly for parents and guardians, and parental involvement is a key factor for student success in providing a way for parents and other stakeholders to learn about their child's school and other public schools in the state. School leaders and building-level administrators are then responsible for distributing the school report cards or snapshots to their school families and community members once they are made available by the state.

School accountability systems have long been the topic of academic research, as well as pedagogical conversations, particularly in the United States. With high-stakes testing as the driving force behind schools' ability to measure and track student achievement, school accountability models fuel "incentives for schools to generate higher performance in academic subjects, and indeed, schools appear to pay attention to the subject matter on which the tests are based" (NCDPI, 2014). Adequately preparing students to tackle core subjects—English language arts (ELA), mathematics, science, and social studies—while increasing their overall achievement in nontested areas, such as electives, foreign language, and physical education, is the universal goal for most school leaders and the educators they work alongside. Using mathematical formulas to derive a letter grade to characterize instructional transformation from year to year adds significant information to an already cumbersome conversation about student achievement. In the state of North Carolina, the school report card is a hefty addition to the discussion, particularly for low-performing schools.

The number on the caller ID of my newly issued school cell indicated that someone at the district's central office was trying to reach me. When I answered, the elementary education director was on the other end and greeted me warmly. She asked if I would be free later that afternoon to stop by the central office before heading home. Our ILT had been putting in so many late hours during the 4-day work weeks in preparation for the year ahead that I welcomed the opportunity to get out of the school building a few minutes early that Thursday. Once I arrived at the central office, I signed in and made my way to my director's office located in the back of the converted Belk building. Sitting down in the chair adjacent to her executive desk, I felt the energy in the room shift slightly as she stated, "Dr. Hemphill, we just received the official data from last year's EOG scores as well as the schools' report cards." It is an odd feeling to know that you are now fully responsible for official data that happened prior to your leadership. It is an even odder feeling to know that the official data does not paint you, your school family, or students in a positive light; however, as she handed me a copy of the official results from across her desk, I was determined at my core that this would be the last conversation of this nature in which FT Elementary would receive such dismal news. "With an overall proficiency of 32.1%, that earned your school a letter grade of 'F,' Dr. Hemphill. Unfortunately—and I know that this happened before you arrived to our district—this is the first 'F' the district has ever had, and it is going to take a lot of hard work to turn this around." I continued to thumb through the pages of subgroup data, proficiency numbers by grade level, and participation specifications before I responded, "It is going to take a lot of hard work, and we have the right team at FT Elementary to make it happen."

The Walmart© Conversation

One of the major challenges facing school leaders and the journey toward the transformation of our nation's public schools is combating the scrutiny and, oftentimes, misinformation that exists among the general populace. Despite the current status or even celebrations that characterize a school's narrative, communal perception plays a significant role in moving a school forward. Anderson et al. (1999) masterfully describes the historical context of the public's consciousness regarding public schools, stating,

> Parents, professionals, students, educators, and the media have long criticized the quality of education delivered by America's public schools system. With the dawn of the Information Age, it is now even easier to share information, and criticisms, with a wide audience on any topic. A trait common among people is a penchant for promulgating "bad news," which makes it even easier to believe that American public schools are failing to educate our children.

School leaders, particularly those who are chosen to turn around failing schools, come face-to-face with the stories, rumors, and gossip that further undergird the bad-news mentality merely by virtue of the school's backstory. These conversations happen sometimes to our faces but most times behind our backs at the grocery store, the pharmacy, the laundromat, the local recreation center, the barbershop, and the salon. Anywhere the community gathers and exchanges information is an opportunity to perpetuate the narrative (both true and untrue) that characterizes a school. Recognizing that this ongoing conversation is indeed occurring, providing context, redirecting erroneous information, and arming one's school community to address these conversations is a critical and necessary step in transforming the conversation in and around the school. As society continues to transform, one understands that not so long ago, people who devoted much of their professional lives to public education were able to simply concentrate on the critical and arduous work before them. These stakeholders knew that the public would, in some sentiment, support their overall efforts to educate students to the best of their ability. That time has passed. School leaders are leading in a much different juncture than the days of old, and there is a battle cry for a different approach to transformation.

Standing in front of the faculty and staff of FT Elementary for the first time, I felt a certain twinge of excitement run through my entire body. There was a great deal of preparation that had gone into this school year's opening meeting: from the card stock cruise ship tickets that had been hand delivered to each individual, to the real seashells from the North Carolina coast that decorated the tables amid fishers' nets and handfuls of sand. Each faculty and staff member was greeted by name by me and our new assistant principal at the door with an energetic, "Welcome aboard FT Elementary Cruises!" And before we lifted our anchor to set sail toward success, no cruise would be ideal unless we all danced down the lido deck to our favorite oldies but goodies! After everyone had taken a turn showing off their moves, I was met with smiles, some leftover giggles from the members of the kindergarten team who did "the bump" down the Soul Train line, and some blank stares from faculty and staff members who were anxiously awaiting this initial address to kick off the school year.

"I want to welcome everyone to the 2015–2016 school year, and I want to thank each and every one of you for your time, energy, ideas, and participation to ensuring that we had a productive summer. Having the opportunity to spend time with you as individuals gave our instructional lead team great insight into who we are as a school family and provided clarity on the potential for this school in the future. Perhaps one of the greatest takeaways from this summer's individual meetings was the level of hope and faith that this faculty and staff possesses in and for our students. There was not one faculty member, one support staff member, community stakeholder, cafeteria employee, or custodian who sat in front of me and used the word 'can't,' 'won't,' or 'failure.' There was not one of you here this morning that utilized the past as a crutch when it comes to making progress this upcoming school year, and, finally, there was not a single FT Elementary family member who communicated to me that this school's past stories would be an excuse for why we cannot write a phenomenal future story—together."

At this point, many of the faculty and staff were nodding their heads in agreement and several were now fixated on the whiteboard behind me, which was covered with a white cloth. I walked over to the corner of the room and strategically placed my hand on the corner of the board. I paused for a moment and before proceeding, I reminded myself that addressing the gigantic dancing purple elephant in the room would be the only way to redirect the teacher lounge talk. I reminded myself that avoiding the conversation that was buzzing in the community would only serve to perpetuate the years of negative discussion that had plagued FT Elementary for years. Finally, I reminded myself that leadership means tackling challenges head-on and moving everyone forward with the vision versus in spite of the vision. I slid my hand to the edge of the chart paper and peeled the cover back to reveal a giant "F" that our team had drawn right in the center. The room fell silent. I pointed at the ominous letter and said, "Two days ago, the state of North Carolina made a declaration regarding our school. For the first time in the history of this school district, there is an 'F' school on their roster based on the North Carolina school report card. Two days ago, our hometown newspaper printed this information for the entire community, and, of course, there has been a lot of conversation surrounding this news, how it happened, and even why it happened. But FT Family, two days ago could be the beginning of one of the greatest success stories in the history of this school and this district. Two days ago, this news gave us an opportunity to change the Walmart conversation. It has happened to all of us. You are in Walmart with a cart filled to the brim with school supplies or one of our students is in Walmart going back-to-school shopping with his or her parents. Someone you know sees you and approaches your cart to greet you. When they look in your cart, they see the No. 2 pencils, notebooks, and reams of loose-leaf paper only to ask, 'What school do you work at?' or 'What school do you go to?' Two days ago, when your response was 'FT Elementary,' it was met with 'Oh, I have heard about that school!' or 'I'm so sorry!' If we want to change the Walmart conversation about our school, it is going to start with us and that means that we are going to have to look at this 'F' as an opportunity to change!"

At this point, I turned back toward the chart paper and grabbed a thick black Sharpie and drew a line from the tip of the failing grade all the way down, instantly turning that "F" into an "A." With as much determination in my voice as I could muster, I turned toward our faculty and staff and asked, "Who is going to help our school turn this 'F' into an 'A'? Who is not going to accept that the students walking in that front door every morning are failures but rather success stories waiting to be written? Who is going to challenge the Walmart conversation head-on and combat each and every rumor with positive news about what is happening in our school with our students and our staff?" Faculty and staff were screaming, "We are!" Some had even stood up at their seats in excitement. But there were some who had tears in their eyes. I would find out later that they were moved with emotion because before this point, they had had no hope. No hope that things at FT Elementary would change. No hope that this would be a school year any different than the last. No hope that they themselves could actually make change happen for the children they so desperately cared for and taught each day. We would all find out very soon that FT Elementary was changing—and it was only the beginning.

One-Minute Challenge:

To change the Walmart conversation about your school, you must know the Walmart conversation. Choose one student leader, one teacher leader, one parent leader, and one community stakeholder and give them 1 minute to tell the story of your school. Ask these stakeholders to tell you about your school as if you were a stranger and allow them to share their perspectives, viewpoints, and experiences in their own unique way. Capture their stories and relay them to your ILT and/or school improvement team. Based on the stories you have collected, what is the current story about your school as a learning community? What common themes are prevalent in the fabric of each of the stories?

One-Minute Post-Pandemic Strategy

COVID-19 has etched itself into the tapestry of every school story in our nation. Undoubtedly, as your school establishes its post-pandemic response and academic strategy to address ever-changing needs, that story will frequently change. As you work with your ILT or school improvement team, ensure that your school plans to touch base with its stakeholders monthly or quarterly. In this way, you can monitor the pulse of your school story and determine how you and your team can best respond to your school's ever-changing needs.

The Needs Assessment

One-Minute Reflection Question:
How do school leaders disaggregate the data of a school in critical condition?

In this chapter, school leaders will dive headfirst into the process of unpacking the historical data of a school in crisis. Charting the course toward success for any school requires that transformational leaders fully understand a school's past. A comprehensive needs assessment marries informal and formal data to paint a clear picture about a particular school's celebrations, challenges, and opportunities for growth. Before delving into the One-Minute Meeting process, school leaders must explore the foundation of their schools holistically and urgently to glean necessary knowledge upon which future decisions will be made. The needs of a school are as unique as fingerprints and DNA characteristic only to that learning environment and community, unable to be replicated, and identifiable only through microscopic lenses.

> *What were the circumstances surrounding their learning environment that set them up for success?*
>
> **—Dr. Hemphill**

A s soon as I located the data notebooks in the back of the conference room, I quickly realized that this would be an arduous task. I still had a few days before my formal onboarding with the school district, but it was apparent that I needed to get a jump start on collecting as much information about FT Elementary as I could. The multicolored tabs of the notebook indicating each grade level were illegible, and some of the pages in the back of the notebook had been haphazardly placed in the torn pocket. I opened the notebook precariously so as not to disturb the sequence of pages, but as soon as I flipped to the first page, a paper-clipped bundle fell to the floor at my feet. "Oh dear!" I thought, "How am I ever going to make sense of these scores?!" While I preferred to have clean data sheets of the previous year's data, I thumbed through the next couple of pages and immediately realized I would have to start from scratch to create a chronological system that would make sense to our ILT. I only had a few days before I would have my first formal meeting with the new assistant principal and instructional facilitator. It was critical that I was as prepared and organized as possible.

I started with the most current data from the previous school year and organized the EOG scores for the third, fourth, and fifth grades based on mathematics and ELA. Then I created tabs for kindergarten and first and second grades and placed their mClass scores from the beginning-of-year, middle-of-year, and end-of-year benchmarks in the back. Upon scanning just the third-grade scores, I immediately felt an overwhelming sense of concern. Each third-grade teacher had approximately 20 to 23 students on their rosters, and I ran my finger down the column of leveled scores, reading them silently to myself. "Level 1, Level 1, Level 2, Level 1, Level 3, Level 1 …" After the first two classes, I stopped scanning and quickly grabbed a Post-it® Note and my iPhone. I scribbled the three EOG averages on the bright yellow Post-it Note and opened the calculator app on my phone to get an average for third-grade ELA: 22%. Only 22% of my third graders (approximately 15 students) were proficient in reading according to the North Carolina EOG. Only 15 students were going into the fourth grade with a solid grasp on the foundational concepts that were necessary for them to build new fourth-grade literacy skills. Only 15 students, according to these scores, had conquered the state gateway of reading on grade level. What did these 15 students experience at FT Elementary in their third-grade year that set them apart from the other almost 50 students who did not pass their ELA EOG? What were the circumstances surrounding their learning environment that set them up for success? How did FT Elementary manage to arrive at the end of the school year with only a handful of third graders crossing the proverbial finish line while so many other third graders were still haphazardly and clumsily running the race? I was about to find out.

Informal Data Versus Formal Data

To gain a holistic perspective on a school's instructional portrait, school leaders should gather as many pieces of informal and formal data as possible. Most commonly, formal data measures a specific piece or segment of the curriculum through predetermined assessments, including quizzes, tests, projects, presentations, etc. School leaders can collect formal data throughout the school year and disaggregate this type of data in multiple ways for their leadership teams, grade levels, and departments. Informal data measures organic interactions, experiences, and observations throughout the school year through teacher-school leader, teacher-teacher, student-teacher, and even student-school leader interactions. As school leaders observe teaching and learning within and throughout the school, informal data can be collected from several domains, including instructional activities, community engagement, strategic planning, and even micropolitical interactions.

Using the informal and formal data collected helps school leaders better navigate the intricacies of school leadership, as well as respond to the stakeholders within the learning community. Penuel et al. (2010) hypothesized in their case study, which focused on the implications of teaching in schools, that "the alignment of the formal and informal aspects of schools as organizations is essential for developing a common vision for reform that can help bring about coordinated instructional change." It is when the informal and formal data are carefully analyzed and aligned with the school improvement goals that a school leader is able to make well-informed, sound decisions that affect the entire learning community. As information is collected, school leaders should develop an organizational system that creates continuity for their teams to easily access and make sense of the information. Whether it is survey responses, standardized test scores, observation and evaluation data, or anecdotal notes from parent and community meetings, the better formal and informal data are organized, the more efficient leadership teams can process and implement instructional changes and policies in a school.

Identifying 3-Year Trends

One way a school leader can begin the process of identifying 3-year trends is to isolate the grade level or stakeholder group that has been historically successful or unsuccessful. Gather the last 3 years of instructional data from a particular stakeholder group (i.e., third grade, band, or Math I). Using the pertinent data associated with this group, begin aligning the data starting with the most current school year and working back 3 years. Look for noticeable changes in student achievement, teachers who outperformed the state average, or even instructional dips in testing participation. While it may seem that these data revelations are small, school leaders working in transitioning learning environments should use these revelations to inform future decisions and instructional conversations with faculty, staff, and leadership. Teacher leaders and support staff who have weathered the course of multiple administrators, particularly in turnaround schools, appreciate the foresight of well-informed school leaders.

In the course of one school year, there are a plethora of factors and incidents that can influence outcomes in a school. Instructionally, there can be mandatory changes in the curriculum at the state, district, and school levels; varying degrees of implementation and interpretation from classroom to classroom; and even personnel changes at the teacher and school leadership levels can impact outcomes. Determining 3-year trends in instructional data helps school leaders distinguish areas of consistency, find opportunities for growth, and challenge areas for the school as a whole. The more trends that school leaders can solidify with data, the less likely they will repeat failures or spend unnecessary time, attention, and resources on less critical areas. Many school districts and states already have available data from standardized tests, national assessments, and statewide reports; however, all data tells a story. School leaders leading schools that are in instructional crisis must establish the protagonists, antagonists, settings, problems, and resolutions associated with their schools' stories over the past 3 years to eventually produce chapters centered on success.

Content Area Data

Whether you work in an elementary, middle, or high school, content area data serves as the pinnacle upon which schools are measured, resources are allocated, and instructional curricula determined. Though it is a long-argued debate that content areas hold more weight, each content area is critical to the make-up of the instructional backbone of a school. When delving into content-area data, school leaders should be clear and precise on the expectations for data analysis. Developing school data teams that are adept at gathering and analyzing data are key factors that lead to rich instructional conversations and impactful outcomes for students and teachers. For each content area, data samples provide an overview of the standards and curriculum covered in a semester, quarter, or over the course of a school year. Arter (2013), in her research article entitled "Assessment for Learning: Classroom Assessment to Improve Student Achievement and Well-Being," thoroughly captures teachers' and school leaders' apprehension with content area data analysis by stating,

> Educators sometimes feel nervous when the concept of sampling arises because it seems highly technical. But sampling is a matter of common sense. It's important to know just how much evidence we need to collect to make a confident conclusion about student achievement. Too much is a waste of time, too little does not provide enough information for good planning. For example, one sample of writing is not enough to determine how well a student writes. One would probably need to sample writing for various audiences and purposes to, really know how well students write. Educators do not need to use fancy models of sampling. All they need is a good understanding of the content they are teaching and an awareness that they need to sample all-aspects of it. (p. 476)

The less intimidating data analysis is for school leaders and their data teams, the higher the probability of having authentic spaces for exploration, conversation, and transformation concerning student achievement.

Behavioral Data

The enrollment at FT Elementary had fluctuated for the past several years because of a multitude of reasons. The surrounding community was full of rental properties and low-income housing, which increased the transiency of our student population throughout the school year, and the dilapidated fish market across the street was rumored to be a high-traffic drug house. New families came to enroll at FT Elementary from the neighboring counties, each with similar comments that could be heard from my office: "Oh, I heard about this school." "Y'all have a lot of bad kids here, don't you?" And the one that made me personally cringe, "We are only coming here because my child needs to be in school, but we are transferring out as soon as possible!" With such negative introductions and conversations happening around FT Elementary, it was no wonder that the expectations of student behavior were dismal at best.

I requested the previous school year's office referral data and worked with our student support team to begin analyzing the trends. We first worked to carefully total up the number of out-of-school suspensions. I explained to the team that any day a student was suspended from school was a day of precious lost instructional time. Because FT Elementary was a school in crisis, we needed to determine how many days our students had spent outside the school building. After careful calculations and data disaggregation, we determined that there were almost 467 out-of-school suspensions the previous school year. In a school with a total of 400 students, this equated to a majority of the students (most of them repeat offenders) being sent home at least once during the school year! Upon further analysis, our team began looking to determine which types of behaviors were most prevalent among FT Elementary students. By a large margin, some of the top contenders were aggressive behavior, disruptive behavior, fighting, and insubordination. And, lastly, I wanted our team to determine *where* these behaviors were occurring. It was critical that we pinpoint the area(s) of the building where behaviors were occurring to develop a more detailed plan for addressing them. We were surprised to learn that according to the data, over 80% of behavior occurred in the one place that should have provided the most engagement, insight, and opportunity for our students: the classroom.

Every Behavior Communicates Something

When adults are frustrated or fed up with a situation or person, they tap into the reservoir of coping mechanisms they have acquired over the years to choose a strategy that allows them to navigate through the experience. Perhaps it is counting to 10 to calm themselves down, daydreaming about a place they would rather be, or even politely excusing themselves from the uncomfortable situation. Whatever the strategy, adults have the luxury of benefiting from learned experiences to help them through life when difficult and unwanted things happen to and around them. Children do not have the luxury of experience. They are forced to attend school for the first formidable years of their lives and make sense of the world based on their limited knowledge and experiences with other humans. It is for these reasons that each one of their behaviors communicates something that teachers and school leaders can use as behavioral data. If a middle school girl cries when it is time for lunch, perhaps she is experiencing anxiety about eating in front of other children because of an eating disorder. If a fifth-grade boy begins acting out each day in his reading block, perhaps he does not want his classmates to find out that he is a poor reader, and he opts instead for being sent to the office to avoid the embarrassment. Each student's behavior is unique to them; however, much like the instructional data that paints an intimate portrait of how the curriculum is interpreted and implemented, behavioral data can lead a school leader to undiscovered trends that can redirect students and help teachers better understand and teach them.

Major Versus Minor Behaviors

Most behaviors in a school can be categorized as major or minor. Major behaviors include fighting, property damage, theft, or even possession of a controlled or illegal item, while minor behaviors involve teasing, taunting, inappropriate language, disrespect, and minor disruptions. The school leader's goal in addressing both major and minor behaviors in a school is to move students toward more autonomous behaviors that result in an increase in self-disciplinary behaviors. According to Bear (2010), "Research shows that self-discipline promotes positive relations with others and a positive school climate, fosters academic achievement, and promotes self-worth and emotional well-being" (p. 46). Addressing major behaviors first allows school leaders to remove costly distractions from the learning environment that take students' attention from learning and teachers' attention from teaching. Major discipline issues also seemingly involve tons of human resources and time, including investigations, correspondence with parents or guardians, follow-up meetings, and, if it is deemed a major reportable offense, law enforcement. While major offenses have the most direct and evident effect on teaching and learning, minor offenses tend to add up if not addressed appropriately as well. If 10 teachers in a school of 400 students write up two students a week for inappropriate language, consider the number of students who have witnessed those 20 students cursing in their learning environment. The effect of that minor behavior can be far-reaching; therefore, a school leader may suggest that the school's guidance counselor work with the identified students on appropriate school language or determine in which grade level the behavior is most prevalent to start a class-wide incentive for not cursing. Major and minor behaviors affect learning environments differently, but the key is to leverage those behaviors to make positive changes for students.

Location, Location, Location

It is not enough to simply address the behaviors that are occurring in a learning environment. Taking the time to ascertain where the behaviors are recurring can provide great insight for school leaders and leadership teams as well. If upon analyzing office referrals for a specified amount of time the data reveals that a majority of the second-grade discipline is happening on the playground, there are a multitude of implications to consider. School leaders should ask questions surrounding appropriate supervision for second-grade students, methods of teaching appropriate playground behavior, and student expectations, as well as master scheduling, to ensure that multiple second-grade classes are not on the playground at the same time. Creating spaces for conversation among the second-grade team and collecting informal data from the teachers will help to solidify the root causes of the behaviors and form productive professional relationships as school leaders and teacher leaders work together to decrease behaviors.

Smith (2014), in his article "Disaggregation of Data in a RtI/PBIS Framework," offers a strategy for school leaders and ILTs in the form of precision statements that allow teams to use discipline data to create "an action plan that would address things to do differently with the students." Precision statements provide measures of accountability for students and teachers, along with opportunities for teaching students new expectations in the process. Through this process, school leaders work closely with stakeholder groups to clearly define the behaviors to create a common language in and among the school and revisit what constitutes those behaviors in the major and minor arena. Using the previous example, if the data revealed that a majority of the second-grade discipline is happening on the playground, then digging deeper to determine the type of office referral would help the team pinpoint the specific behavior to be addressed. If fighting constituted over 80% of the second-grade referrals on the playground, then the school leader and data team would work to ensure that the second-grade teaching team and support staff possessed the same definition for fighting and altercations. School leaders would then create clear delineations of major and minor physical altercations (i.e., fist fighting versus tapping) and come to a consensus with the stakeholder team. Lastly, a precision statement would be developed, for example, to decrease the office referrals for second-grade fights on the playground by 35% within the next 2 weeks. Student behavior and discipline data would be monitored closely, and the precision statement would then be analyzed and necessary adjustments made at the end of the 2 weeks. Behavioral data analysis can provide great insight and next steps for school leaders and their leadership teams to deeply analyze safety measures and develop a plan to remove the barriers to students' success.

Measuring Mental Health

Mental health is a widely talked about issue in the educational arena and a topic that has taken center stage on the world scene. While there is still much work to be done and research to be conducted around this robust topic, most schools and educators recognize that the work of acknowledging and supporting students' mental health is a vital part of whole-child education in the 21st century (Thiers, 2018). When completing a comprehensive needs assessment of a school, school leaders should take into consideration existing cases of students who require mental health resources and support, as well as students or groups of students who are also in need of such services. Although the continuum of support is vast and varies from state to state and district to district, it is well worth the time and attention necessary to ascertain students' needs to ensure that a plan is in place and adhered to. Until socioemotional health is addressed as a school, students cannot be expected to focus their full attention on teaching and learning. It is the school leader's responsibility to mobilize knowledgeable teams to not only disaggregate the data surrounding mental health impact in the learning community but also assemble available mental health supports to address specific needs. Kaffenberger (2011) proposes that to meet the mental health needs of all students successfully "may require new methods and service delivery models, and will be dependent on collaboration among all of the adults in the child's environment and access to mental health professionals in the local community" (p. 325). There is a long-quoted saying in the educational community: "You cannot take care of the Bloom stuff until you take care of the Maslow stuff." And when it comes to the mental health and well-being of our students, that is a saying that bears truth.

Physical Data

FT Elementary was one of the oldest schools in the district. In fact, it was one of the oldest schools in the surrounding counties with its rich history dating back to the days of integration. Erected in the 1950s, its once pristine brick-and-mortar exterior had faded to a worn, somewhat patchy exterior. The specially erected storage facilities on the property were now overgrown with kudzu and vines. And the shiny hallways and classrooms that were home to hundreds of local middle and high school alumni were now bordered by cracked pavements and frosty windows that braced for the pitter-patter of 400 elementary-aged feet each day. Upon first glance, the exterior did little to inspire onlookers to believe that teaching and learning were thriving inside the building; however, the physical edifice itself possessed character and had become a fixture in the local community. For weeks and weeks after I was named the new principal at FT Elementary, I received dozens of phone calls, text messages, and visitors who were local alumni wishing to regale me with their fond memories of their time in what was once Fannie Tyson High School, then Fannie Tyson Middle School, and now Fannie Tyson Elementary. There was even a local alumni group consisting of about 50–60 individuals who hosted a well-attended fundraiser each year to raise monies for the building that housed my now almost 400 scholars. Last year, I was told that they raised enough money to have brand-new signage affixed to the front of the school donning the name Fannie Tyson Elementary in bright, shiny white letters so that everyone in the neighborhood could read the school name. It was evident that FT Elementary held a special place in the community's heart.

The interior of the building was a different story altogether. Upon entering the foyer of the school, visitors were met with an antiquated double-glass door that served as a fail lock to keep intruders in the main office area. The pixelated glass appeared scratched but was in fact cleaned and buffed daily by the school's amazing custodial team. Making one's way down the hall, the big cinder block walls were a putrid shade of white, although the fingerprints from little hands and footprints of muddy feet along the base distracted from the off-white hue. I peeked into several classrooms during my initial walk-through to get a feel for the size of the classrooms and was immediately overwhelmed by the immense amount of clutter and lack of organization on the built-in shelves. Literacy games and math manipulatives were spilling out of cabinets, many of the walls were decorated with multicolored word flash cards, and in many of the classrooms, desks were haphazardly arranged in U-shapes or semi-straight rows in all directions. "It seems as if it is not just the instruction that requires a makeover," I thought to myself. If we were going to transform FT Elementary into a school of excellence and the best school to learn in and work for in this district, the building was going to have to undergo a transformation as well.

Shifting Perspective

Very rarely do school leaders have the option or even the ability to dictate specific capital outlay projects or budgets to completely innovate the physical building. Even principals who are chosen to open brand-new buildings often find after starting the school year that there are small nuances that were not considered by the architects or contractors that they would have altered to accommodate a particular stakeholder group or educational program. One of the greatest challenges facing school leaders who direct learning communities housed in older construction is determining how to repurpose and redesign the given space to meet the needs of 21st-century learning and learners. Ives (2018) recognizes this conundrum and offers school leaders hope in her academic article "Thinking Inside the Box—Transforming Existing Buildings into Outstanding 21st Century Learning Environments" by stating, "The challenge is breathing new life into existing buildings by transforming spaces for educational purposes. Using the building as our silent partner, we can look for clues to determine where to modify, carve out, remove, and add elements to mold the existing building to its new use." While older facilities come with a laundry list of necessary upgrades and a wish list of new furniture and fixtures, school leaders should purposefully search for tangible, realistic, and cost-effective ways to convert spaces to begin the physical manifestation of transformation.

Oftentimes, school leaders with facility issues also combat deeply rooted mind-sets and perspectives about the building itself. Perhaps the school was erected years ago and has a heavy historical context in the community. Altering even a part of a school building of this nature requires meetings with respective local organizations or alumni associations, as well as district permissions and possibly school board approval. Transforming a school starts with a school leader who is able to guide the appropriate stakeholders effectively toward new outlooks and potential opportunities that align with a transformed vision and direction. Ives (2018) purports that older facilities can indeed be transformed; however, it requires careful scrutiny and precise direction to determine how the space can be reconfigured to meet specific needs:

> An existing building must be carefully analyzed to determine if it is conducive for educational use. The building structure and column spacing—components that are not easily modified—must be evaluated to determine if they lend themselves to flexible space planning. Existing mechanical and electrical systems must be inspected to determine if they can be modified to suit the new interior layout and program. Often, building systems are at the end of their useful life and replacing them with new, efficient equipment is beneficial.

While certain stakeholders, including teacher leaders inside the building, may not understand or agree with the critical transformation in a school building, there is no denying that a productive and purposeful learning environment leads to productive and purposeful teaching and learning. It may require a school leader to think creatively and innovatively about the approach; however, shifting the perspective regarding physical space can lead to much-needed and urgent changes for schools in crisis.

Conducting a Facility Walk-Through

As a school leader in a building, conducting a thorough facility walk-through allows one to see the building with fresh eyes and a renewed perspective. In order to begin the process of transformation, identifying problem areas and developing smart solutions allows leadership teams to guide students and teachers toward embracing and using the building in new and creative ways. Prior to preparing for an initial facility walk-through, school leaders should work with their leadership or school improvement team (SIT) to create a unified organizational vision for the school itself. This is an opportunity to address obvious structure concerns, safety hazards, and malfunctioning equipment, as well as to determine how these issues affect teaching and learning for students and teacher leaders. Throughout this discussion, school leaders can work to establish honest and transparent opportunities for conversations on the realities of capital outlay budgets and necessary financial resources to address specific physical deficits. Allowing the leadership team to weigh in on these types of conversations develops distributive leadership throughout the building and helps to shift the perspective on addressing the physical space. Leadership teams can also create wish lists in this initial phase by focusing intently on schoolwide instructional goals and determining how the building can be altered to help the school achieve those goals. Wish lists can include everything from new playground equipment, educational murals in the hallways, flexible seating in classrooms, or landscaping around the entire exterior of the building. By having a clear focus as to how these alterations lead to increased morale, better classroom management, or serve an educational focus, it allows the team to conduct a resolute facility walk-through.

Once the organizational vision is established, school leaders can assemble the team to conduct the actual walk-through. It is a good idea to include the lead custodian or member of the custodial team to establish transparency and continuity in achieving the organizational vision. Custodians are extremely important stakeholders in the school, as they are building experts and can offer amazing insight into the specifics and particulars regarding the physical edifice. It is recommended to include a member of the district custodial or maintenance department as well to add a macrolens and perspective to any requested changes or urgent safety concerns. Together as a team, walk the exterior and interior of the building, leaving no corner or crevice unturned or uncovered. Make a list of immediate concerns and assign someone on the team with a date for follow-up, by which time the concern should be addressed. For larger wish list issues, request a formal meeting with the district facilities or maintenance director after the facility walk-through to establish reasonable time lines and money sources to match the organizational vision. Transforming the physical space for teaching and learning can be a tangible and immediate manifestation of the transformation happening within teaching and learning in a school. Being strategic and intentional allows school leaders to maximize their efforts to provide students with a learning space that breeds productivity!

One-Minute Challenge:
This one-minute challenge will involve your entire ILT or SIT. Assign each member of the team (or organize small teams) to one of the following areas: formal school data, informal school data, content area data, behavioral data, mental health data, and facility walk-through. Each member or team is tasked with gleaning specific data in their area and creating a one-minute report to share their results/findings. Use the one-minute report data to begin creating a holistic perspective on a school's instructional, cultural, and physical portrait and to guide discussion about priority areas for your learning community.

One-Minute Post-Pandemic Strategy
Research continues to confirm that the impact of the pandemic will have far-reaching effects on the overall mental health of our nation's students. As you complete the school's needs assessment, advocate and plan proactively to secure the necessary mental health resources and human capital to respond to students' needs.

3

The Mission Statement

One-Minute Reflection Question:
How do school leaders ensure that their schools' mission statements add purpose and value to their daily operations and interactions?

In this chapter, school leaders come face-to-face with their schools' purpose for being. Examining a school's mission statement provides school leaders with a clear path to understanding how students, teachers, parents, and the community perceive the school as a whole. The mission statement should serve as more than mere words on the cover sheet of the school improvement plan but also provide a school community with a solid framework upon which all stakeholders can navigate the daily work that happens in the building, who the work is impacting, and what value the work brings for all involved. Throughout this One-Minute Meeting journey, the school leader will connect all interactions, questions, and data from the perspective of the school's mission statement. There are multiple moving parts and moving entities that make up a thriving, successful learning community. A school leader's main task is to create the conditions upon which all of those moving parts are focused solely on the school's mission.

> *I'm not really sure what our school's mission statement says.*
> **—The SIT Chair**

I will never forget my first SIT meeting at FT Elementary. It was the week after our epic opening meeting, and everyone was on a proverbial high. With the start of the school year in just a few days, teacher leaders in the building felt a rush of energy they had not felt in a long time. Many of the veteran teachers stopped by my office between trips to the main office and the instructional supply closet simply to say how excited they were for the year ahead. Several were astounded that we had actually addressed the real issues and not sugarcoated the meeting with empty promises and nonrealistic goals. One teacher even wrote a short email to our ILT stating,

> *"Thank you for giving me permission to be myself again. It's been a long time since I looked forward to the start of the school year!"*

With this type of energy reverberating through the hallways, I instructed our lead team to ensure that they kept a pulse on their specific areas over the following weeks. If we wanted to begin transforming the culture and morale at FT Elementary, it would require intentional and consistent monitoring to make urgent adjustments throughout the remainder of the year.

The newly elected SIT members made their way into the media center armed with laptops, new notebooks, and freshly sharpened pencils. This was the first time in quite a while that the entire faculty and staff had voted on its SIT representatives after our lead team had meticulously reviewed the state requirements during the opening meeting rotations. Our assistant principal had created an online ballot with the names of all eligible faculty members and made it available to our staff. Once all the votes had been counted and the new SIT members announced, our team sent them a congratulatory email with a preliminary outline of their new duties and responsibilities, along with the dates of SIT meetings for the remainder of the year. Every first Tuesday of the month, we gathered to discuss, analyze, and develop policies, procedures, activities, and events that would chart the course to success for our school. It was no small task, but having a team of dedicated, energetic stakeholders at the table was the first step in the right direction.

I welcomed everyone to our first SIT meeting of the year and begin handing out colored copies of last year's school improvement plan. Any time we had important documents to disperse from the main office, I requested that they be on brightly colored paper. This would help our teachers and ILT to distinguish important documents from the sea of white copy paper that abounds in a school.

"As we get started this morning, I want to ask this team, 'What is FT Elementary's mission?'"

Frantic blank stares began bouncing from table to table as teacher leaders looked at one another in desperation. A few SIT members began to answer softly, but their mumbled words faded into a trail of inquisitive huffs and gestures. Even our assistant principal buried her head into her laptop to avoid making eye contact with me.

"What does this school stand for? What is our purpose as a school when we teach in our classrooms and those students walk through our doors?" I offered to help their thinking along. I walked over to our newly appointed SIT chair and asked, "What does our school's mission statement say?"

She looked at me and laughed nervously before responding, "I'm not really sure what our school's mission statement says."

By this point, a couple of our teacher leaders had figured out that the mission statement was plastered on the cover sheet of the school improvement plan I had just handed out, and many were raising their hands to provide the answer to the question I had posed almost 5 minutes before. I walked back to the front of the group and said, "I wanted to make a point. It does not matter what our mission statement says if it is not something that is ingrained into everything we do at this school. Each of you *work* here, and yet you are not able to state the mission. That means it is not a part of our everyday thinking in this building. If we do not know the mission, then how can we expect parents and community members to support it and get behind us in our efforts? We have some work to do."

Can Anyone Recite the Mission Statement?

It is not uncommon for a school's mission statement to take a backseat over time. Particularly in schools that experience lots of teacher and school leader turnover, the focus tends to shift toward retention and establishing consistency versus ensuring that the new leader and new staff are focused on the school's mission. According to Fuller (2012) in his analysis of why principals leave schools, it is a phenomena that "plague[s] low-performing schools and, in the case of principal turnover, afflict[s] a wide range of schools regardless of performance or school demographics." With each new school leader comes a ritualistic process of discovering and uncovering that has deep-rooted effects on the teacher leaders, students, parents, and communities that remain. The policies and procedures that were ingrained within stakeholders now have a new inter-pretation. The instructional focus and strategy that teachers learned to implement now need tweaking. The methods of communication that parents and families had grown accustomed to is now scrutinized based on the new methods. It is an ongoing cycle of change and inconsistencies that are unfortunately prevalent in the schools that require the most stability.

Despite the academic research, which argues that one way to improve low-performing schools is to replace its leaders and to do so with greater frequency, the reality suggests that there are serious downsides (Fuller, 2012). One such disadvantage is that the mission gets lost and often misinterpreted in the shuffle to reorganize and rebrand with each new principal. The mission statement brings value to the work that happens within the school itself. When students and teachers experience frequent fluctuations in that value versus the consistent message that a mission statement provides, a lack of buy-in follows. Teachers are left to infuse their teaching with their own interpretations of why teaching is valuable, and students are left to continue asking why it is so. In the event that school leaders do continue their tenure for more than a year or two, it is an extremely arduous task to regain momentum with a new mission statement because of the lack of trust that the mission itself will stick around.

One of the key ways that school leaders can combat this lack of assurance in schools is to employ collective and shared leadership practices as frequently as pos-sible, particularly as it relates to establishing or reestablishing a mission statement. Burkhauser et al. (2012) conducted a study entitled "First-Year Principals in Urban School Districts: How Actions and Working Conditions Relate to Outcomes" and conclusively affirm that

> rather than changing everything or making independent decisions, princi-pals and teachers reported that principals were more successful in garnering

teacher buy-in when they consulted with staff to gain information on perceived strengths and weaknesses at the school. Beyond the initial diagnosis, these principals honored school philosophies by incorporating them into their school-improvement strategies.

Developing strong teams of teacher leaders, parent leaders, community leaders, and even student leaders is an effective way to ensure that school traditions, instructional methodologies, mission statements, and important policies remain at the forefront of all decisions. With consistent voices around the table, school leaders can increase their ability to keep a school's purpose and its mission alive!

Developing the Mission

After a school leader has gone through the process of assembling an effective team of stakeholders, it is then time to begin developing the mission or disaggregating the old mission. Establishing cohesiveness from the inception of this process will allow stakeholders to deliver similar messages and updates to various groups within the learning community, which is key as the school leader and leadership team begins the process of transformation. Gabriel and Farmer (2009) allude to this critical assurance, stating, "Whatever the context, the point is the same: if a group wants to move forward, it needs to develop an understood, agreed-on purpose." Determining the purpose of the mission statement is as significant as determining the purpose of the work that happens in a school. School leaders should allow the team to spend time discussing what the school currently stands for, including how various stakeholders perceive the school as a whole. Preliminary questions to guide this discussion include the following:

- What type of educational experience are students in our school having?

- What type of professional experience are teacher leaders in our school having?

- How do community members describe our school?

- What is the narrative our learning community tells about our school as it pertains to our mission?

- What are some keywords that currently and accurately describe our school as it relates to teaching and learning?

It is important to be honest at the onset of this process. To create an atmosphere of honesty and transparency, school leaders and leadership teams should establish norms that help to create a safe space for stakeholders to freely respond to questions and engage in authentic discussion. While creating a culture of trust and respect in a school community takes time, school leaders can model the desired behaviors and expectations with key teams, particularly those tackling critical tasks, such as development of the mission statement. When students and teacher leaders are able to observe school leaders exhibiting honesty and transparency in and among the school, it truly helps to bring the mission statement to life versus an arbitrary mission statement that is rarely discussed or referenced.

After tackling key questions, such as those mentioned earlier, the team will begin creating a mission statement that will drive the school forward. Gabriel and Farmer (2009) eloquently offered a definition for mission statements: "Mission statements are the 'how-to' statements or action plans that help schools achieve their vision. They prompt change and growth. The mission is the touch point that can help you determine whether what should be happening is in fact happening." The process of creating the mission statement is an excellent window of opportunity for school leaders to inspect what they expect in all key areas of the learning community, including revisiting those areas that were previously discussed during the needs assessment. Beginning with those critical areas in which the lead team has already analyzed and discussed formal and informal data provides a practical springboard for conversation and development. The following are a few effective starter questions to promote deep discussions on key needs assessment areas.

Informal Versus Formal Data

What key pieces of informal data do we want to monitor as a school? When will strategic teams analyze these pieces of data and create action steps to address opportunities for improvement?

Which informal processes in our building are tied directly to our mission? Do these processes need to be revisited or redesigned to increase our school's efficacy? If so, how?

What key pieces of formal data do we want to monitor as a school? When will strategic teams analyze these pieces of data and create action steps to address opportunities for improvement?

Which formal processes in our building affect the majority of our school's stakeholders? Do these processes need to be revisited or redesigned to increase our school's efficacy? If so, how?

Identifying 3-Year Trends

Based on our school's needs assessment, what are some key celebrations in our 3-year trends? What are some critical opportunities for improvement in our 3-year trends?

When we put a stake in the ground 3 years from now, where do we want to be as a school? Who are the stakeholder groups that will assist us in accomplishing that mission? What are the key policies and processes that will guide our steps to achieving that mission?

Content Area Data

Based on our school's needs assessment, what are areas of celebration in our content data? What are some critical opportunities for improvement in our content data?

As we develop our mission statement, which content areas do we want to focus on as a learning community to align our physical, human, and financial resources toward accomplishing that mission?

What will be the primary vehicle through which stakeholder groups will increase their impact in those content areas?

When will strategic teams analyze content data and create action steps to address opportunities for improvement?

Behavioral Data

Based on our school's needs assessment, what are areas of celebration in our behavioral data? What are some critical opportunities for improvement in our behavioral data?

As we consider our mission statement, what are key expectations that we want to develop for various stakeholder groups? How will those expectations directly affect desired behaviors in our learning community?

What will be the primary vehicle through which stakeholder groups will be introduced to, practice, and measure behavioral expectations in our school?

When will strategic teams analyze behavioral data and create action steps to address opportunities for improvement?

Mental Health

Based on our school's needs assessment, what areas of mental health significantly affect stakeholders in our school?

What processes currently exist that support our mission as it relates to addressing mental health? Do these processes need to be revisited or redesigned to increase our school's efficacy? If so, how?

What processes do not currently exist that we must create to support our mission as it relates to addressing mental health? How will we advocate for, fund, and design these processes to increase our school's efficacy?

Physical Data and Facilities

Based on our school's needs assessment, what are areas of celebration in our physical data and facilities? What are some critical opportunities for improvement in our physical data and facilities?

As we consider our mission statement, what physical areas of our school must we focus on improving or redesigning to accomplish our mission?

How do we ensure that our physical space and facilities support the ever-changing needs of our school's stakeholder groups? How will we advocate for, fund, and design learning spaces to increase our school's efficacy?

Assigning individuals from SIT to each of these sections is an effective way to tackle this process of establishing a focus for the mission statement. Allowing small groups to work collaboratively, gather key artifacts, speak to other stakeholders in the building, and then create short, but powerful, presentations on their findings allows common themes to organically emerge from the discussions. Mission statements are the road maps schools use to navigate to their desired destinations. Creating transparent processes for feedback and collaborations on key areas ensures that all stakeholders arrive at that destination safely.

Marketing the Mission

Once the mission statement has been developed and agreed upon by the team, it is time to create a marketing strategy. In much the same manner as businesses and organizations create marketing strategies when they are rebranding a popular product or service, school leaders must lead the initiative of ensuring that all stakeholder groups know and understand the new mission statement. Delisio (2008) offers valuable insight in her article "Easy Ways to Market Your Schools" by stating, "Urban schools cope with complex issues, so the more the staff, the press, and the public understand about a district, the easier it can be to build support. It's also very important to have good internal communications, and arm employees with information about the school system or schools, so everyone knows what's going on. It reduces misinformation." Whether a rural, urban, or suburban school, providing as much information as possible to stakeholder groups extends the level of transparency from leadership and allows the mission to begin absorbing into the new culture of the learning community. When students, teacher leaders, parents, community members, and district personnel can speak about a school's mission effortlessly, then the mission has been strategically marketed in multiple ways so as to brand the school based on its purpose and goals.

Announcing the new mission statement can be a big event that involves all stakeholder groups either at the start of a new school year or during a special day or month in the school's history. Perhaps a school leader will choose to unveil the mission statement during a school assembly in which parents, guardians, local businesses, and school board members have been invited. Or perhaps school leaders and their team come up with an innovative way to reveal the mission statement on social media by going live on Instagram or Facebook. Social media is one of the leading means of communication in the 21st century, and it is a proven fact that the preferred method of retrieving news and new information is through a social media platform. Use student talents and ideas to build anticipation for the special day by making announcements, creating digital flyers, and changing the school's marquee approximately 2 weeks prior to the kickoff to ensure that all stakeholders are notified well in advance. Let your students and teacher leaders shine by allowing them to create short commercials and skits that depict their excitement about the new mission statement. When developing the program, invite the strategic team that completed the needs assessment to the table, along with parents and guardians to have representation from all facets of the learning community. School leaders should also be encouraged to adopt a hashtag that can be applicable throughout the school year. Hashtags are memorable and impactful as they draw out the significance of a school's mission with two or three key words. They can be used on social media, in print advertisement for events and activities during the school year, to describe stellar teaching and learning, and even on T-shirts, pennants, school supplies, and school memorabilia designs!

Marketing the school mission statement not only transcends announcing the new purpose and goals for the school but also requires that it becomes stitched into the fabric of every interaction in the learning community. School leaders should assess opportunities throughout the course of the day to consistently model the mission as well as hold stakeholders accountable for modeling it. If the mission statement delineates that students are to become problem solvers and solution seekers, then school leaders must hold teacher leaders accountable for implementing rigor and relevance into their instruction to challenge students' thinking. If the mission statement calls for high levels of integration across the content areas to develop the whole child, then school leaders must hold student support services accountable for modeling the mission through schoolwide socioemotional programs. Carving out time during the instructional day to model the mission is a strategic marketing strategy that allows stakeholder groups to maximize the instructional day and removes barriers to access training and resources. Work intently with the lead instructional team to create professional learning community (PLC) schedules that allow for teacher leaders to model the mission through instruction and team building. Schedule principal-parent breakfast hours throughout the semester to sit down with parents and guardians from various grade levels, departments, and athletic teams to discuss how the school can partner with them to model the mission. Using the One-Minute Meeting process will bring each school leader face-to-face with their most important client—the student body—to engage in critical conversation about their experience in the school. If the mission statement is not purposeful, focused, and embedded in their school's culture, the most important stakeholder in the learning community will reveal it!

One-Minute Challenge:

The school mission statement is a mantra that should be ingrained into the fabric of the school. Work with your ILT to select seven to 10 teacher leaders in the building and develop a schedule to provide them with classroom coverage for 15 minutes on a predetermined school day. Meet with the team of teacher leaders and provide them with a copy of the school's current mission statement. Let them know that they have been selected to do 1-minute mission walk-throughs in various parts of the building during their coverage times. Their goal is to observe whether the school's mission statement is evident during their 1-minute walk-through based on student-teacher interactions, teaching and learning, classroom culture, and even physical space. Schedule a time after school to meet with the team of teacher leaders so they can share their walk-through data and begin discussing next steps toward editing the current mission statement or creating a new one.

One-Minute Post-Pandemic Strategy

As the educational world began to shift and pivot in light of COVID-19, the global spotlight came down on educators and their immense contribution and commitment to guiding future generations in their educational pursuits. Parents and families, many for the first time, found themselves as in-home educators, tutors, and instructional specialists. As you and your ILT or school improvement team work to develop and market your school's mission statement, remind the team to ensure that parents and families are well-represented and supported as critical stakeholders in supporting all students' education.

PART 2　THE STUDENTS

Students as Stakeholders

One-Minute Reflection Question:
How can school leaders begin to capitalize on the perspective of student stakeholders to help transform their schools?

In this chapter, school leaders embark on the process of challenging the status quo within their learning communities. Delving into the importance of student stakeholders in a school can offer school leaders and their teams immense insight into how teaching and learning are affecting their most important customers: students! Each and every day, students bring their likes, dislikes, experiences, cultures, creeds, knowledge, and insight through the front door and head into classrooms, living the best lives afforded to them. What does the school look like through their eyes? How does the teaching that takes place in their classrooms affect their thinking? Why does understanding their interpretation of what happens daily in school matter to school leaders? The One-Minute Meeting journey was created and designed with students in mind. To involve students fully in this process, school leaders must understand the why behind this transformative strategy.

> *It's time to start listening to our students as stakeholders in their education.*
>
> **—Dr. Hemphill**

I t was a crisp autumn day in October, and I was making my way to a kindergarten class on our campus. It had taken a few months, but our lead instructional team had finally gotten into the stride of spending the majority of our time in classrooms. My assistant principal and I tag teamed being available in the main office. If I was conducting walk-throughs, she would cover the phone calls, impromptu parent visits, and cafeteria duty. If she was scheduled to do observations, I would pick up the mantle. Transformation is truly about teamwork, and I could see that our team members were becoming empowered to operate in their areas of expertise. Our motto was "be where the students are." To start the transformation process, the classroom was our first and most critical priority to determine the changes that needed to be made. If our team did not spend quality time in classrooms, we could not help FT Elementary improve.

I stepped outside from the main building into the breezeway, and I immediately felt cool air on my face. For a moment, everything was quiet, and all I could hear was the crunch of freshly fallen leaves under my heels. I was grateful for the brief moment of silence. It had been a whirlwind 3 months since I was charged with the task of leading FT Elementary, and I was honestly proud and grateful for the amazing team of educators at our school. Students, teachers, parents, and even the district office consistently commented on the "new feel" throughout the building, and the energy that our team had been intentional on preserving seemed to grow with each passing school day. Teachers were baffled that the needs and concerns they raised to SIT were met with swift action and necessary changes in implementation. Parents were welcomed with pomp, circumstance, and unparalleled customer service in our newly outfitted main office. And the students were beginning to realize that *something* was different at FT Elementary this year.

About a week into the school year, I was standing at the front door, along with our school nurse and social worker, greeting each of our little ones as they traveled to the cafeteria for breakfast. I could hear someone calling my name. "Dr. Hemphill! Dr. Hemphill, you have to see this!" When I looked down the hall, our school's pre-K teacher was racing past second and third graders, waving what appeared to be a newspaper in her hands. When she reached the front door, she shoved the paper at me and began frantically pointing at an editorial written on the third page. Her excitement was overwhelming, but I was able to make out the headline: "Student Ready to Soar."

To the editor:

I am a fifth grader at FT Elementary School. For years, I thought I wanted to get my fifth-grade year over with so that I could go to middle school, but my mind has recently changed.

Why? I thought you'd never ask.

We have the most awesome principal and teachers in the universe! Our principal, Dr. Mary Hemphill, is the best principal. She makes sure we are learning and not being slack on our work. She comes in each morning with a smile and when I see her, I know I am going to have a great day. Dr. Hemphill and all of my teachers are very positive, caring, considerate, loving, honest, professional, and willing to help me and all of the students in our school.

I am so excited to get up every morning for school.

Yes, it has been only a little over a week, but I know this year will only get better. I am looking forward to the best year ever as I plan to SOAR, be positive, make good grades and obey all of my teachers.

Braxley Compton
5th Grader
FT Elementary

I failed to hold back tears as I took the first steps in the direction of Braxley's fifth-grade classroom. Braxley was a model student on all accounts, but the effort that he put forth to write this letter and have it published in our local newspaper was astonishing. With the newspaper still in hand and tears on my cheeks, I rounded the corner to Ms. Cannady's classroom and spotted Braxley at his desk tackling his morning assignment. Ms. Cannady warmly greeted me with her usual smile and good morning. I asked her if I might interrupt for a moment to which she replied, "Of course." I stepped to the front of the class, and said, "Good morning everyone! Today, it brings me great pleasure to announce that we are in the presence of a local celebrity and author. Our very own Braxley Compton has written a letter to the editor of our local newspaper, and it was published this morning! Braxley, it brings me great joy to be your principal, but we are even more excited to know that you and your classmates love going to our school. Thank you for taking the time to write such a beautiful letter. Class, let's give Braxley a huge round of applause!" As the class erupted in cheers and clapping, I realized that the shift had begun. The same newspaper that just weeks before had published an in-depth article about FT Elementary's F letter grade was now focusing on the small but significant changes that were taking place in our building. The best part, however, was that it was through the perspective of our most important stakeholders: our students.

Abandoning the Top-Down Approach

As the landscape of public education continues to evolve, so does the leadership and vision required to meet the needs of this ever-changing academic platform. "Most school organizations are facing a dynamic environment characterized by rapid social changes, educational policies, and globalization" (Hsiao & Chang, 2011). No longer is academic research focusing solely on school leadership required to lead our 21st-century students and educators toward success; rather, it is focused on the plethora of factors that inform the development of thriving learning communities across our nation. While much of the educational research on leadership and vision speaks to the development of strategies, pedagogies, and leadership preparation for school leaders, there are deficiencies in the literature on student leaders and their role as critical stakeholders based on their own perceptions of school. For transformational school leaders who seek to embolden students as vital voices in the transformation, building schools as learning communities with students at the center is the place to start. According to Senge (2012), "All this is only feasible when we are all willing to rethink basic assumptions about how schools work. Early on, pioneers like those in

Tucson realized that systems thinking had to be connected with enabling students to apply the systems tools to truly meaningful problems—and that this meant changes in the school culture, starting with how the adults worked with one another." When students are authentically capable of articulating how the learning works outside the walls of the classroom and are organically engaging with content in meaningful, valuable ways, then schools transcend from mere brick-and-mortar buildings to live laboratories of learning.

The problem with modern-day academics, research-based strategies, and field-tested pedagogies is that too few revolve around how student stakeholders perceive their learning communities. For schools to truly transform into student-centered environments, school leaders must move intently and expeditiously toward innovative solutions that meticulously place students in the center of it all. When students are positioned to experience, discuss, and analyze their experiences as learners, thinkers, and stakeholders in the school, change happens from the inside out. Senge (2012) went on to purport that a new paradigm requires all stakeholders to work together to create newly defined relationships with newly defined expectations: "It will take leadership from the very place that we look least frequently—the students themselves. Make no mistake. The students are ready for the change." Abandoning the traditional top-down approach means school leaders walking hand in hand with student leaders to help redefine what school looks like from the bottom up. For years, school leaders have evaluated, assessed, discussed, and analyzed prevalent stakeholders from the teacher leaders to community leaders who directly impact their buildings. Principals across the country have logged hundreds of thousands of hours completing formal observations of teachers' lessons, walked hundreds of thousands of steps conducting instructional walk-throughs, and spent hundreds of thousands of hours planning Parent-Teacher Organization meetings, curriculum nights, and parent-teacher conferences. However, what is the real effect of these efforts on student achievement? What effect did that science lesson truly have on the students? How did the walk-through feedback improve learning conditions for the students on that grade level? Why not simply ask them?!

Throughout the decades of formal public education, there have been countless policies, laws, and entities that have, to no avail, tried to bring about widespread educational reform. Hipp and Huffman (2000) asserted, "Many governance structures have been designed to empower a greater number of staff in decision making, yet students fail to reap the benefits." From the Elementary and Secondary Education Act of 1965 to No Child Left Behind in 2001 all the way to the current Every Student Succeeds Act put into effect in 2017, the data affirms that there still exists a widening student achievement gap, an overrepresentation of minorities identified with exceptional needs, and scores of students graduating from high school ill prepared for the real world, having no basic foundational skills. Over the years, the one constant that has defined public education is the student. They come to schools each and every day, sitting in desks or at tables and benches or crisscrossed, apple sauced on square tiles or pillows. Each of them carries the experiences of the first formidable years of their lives in elementary school, the topsy-turvy hormonal years of middle school, or the first visions of college life and their future careers in high school. School leaders know that parents are sending the very best children they have to our learning communities. It is time to shift the leadership paradigm and allow the best to lead the change.

The One-Minute Meeting
Conceptual Framework

The One-Minute Meeting process requires school leaders to reconceptualize their approach to data analysis as it relates to transforming their learning communities. No longer can standardized tests and assessments, formal observations, benchmarks, and working conditions surveys serve as the cornerstones for formidable data that informs the state of teaching and learning in schools. Instead, school leaders will reposition their focus through this process on their number-one customer—the student—and use their experiences through their eyes to make necessary and urgent changes within the school itself. To conceptualize a holistic understanding of students as stakeholders in learning communities, four major constructs are analyzed: transformational leadership, student stakeholders, shared vision, and schools as learning communities.

Transformational Leadership

Within this conceptual framework, transformational leadership and the tenets therein are intricately woven into every fiber of learning communities. Transformational leadership enhances an organization by raising the values of its members, motivating them to go beyond self-interest to embrace organizational goals, and redefining their needs to align with the organizational mission (Ross & Gray, 2006). School leaders who motivate faculty and staff to develop a deep understanding of the school's overall mission and vision to educate all students help them reevaluate their own biases and values (Kark, Shamir, & Chen, 2003). This type of transformational leadership allows the school leader to articulate a strong vision of curriculum and instruction and emotional and social well-being for students, as well as mobilizes faculty and staff to buy into the vision. Leithwood, Jantzi, and Steinbeck (1999) identified eight dimensions of transformational leadership: (1) identifying and articulating a vision, (2) fostering the acceptance of group decision-making goals, (3) providing an appropriate role model, (4) having high-performance expectations, (5) providing individual support, (6) providing intellectual stimulation, (7) offering contingent reward, and (8) managing by exception. These eight constructs help school leaders navigate the sometimes choppy and treacherous waters of transformation toward unparalleled success for students, teacher leaders, and the entire learning community. The One-Minute Meeting construct is just such a transformational effort, as it allows each individual student to have a voice in their learning, positions the school leader and instructional team to truly determine if the vision and mission are actualized throughout the school, and, lastly, provides multiple opportunities for high expectations to be communicated and modeled.

Student Stakeholders

While the formal research on students as stakeholders is scant, the academic world is beginning to see a shift in the scholastic discussion around the role of students in their own education, particularly in the 21st century. Institutions of higher learning and organizations centered primarily on the student voice purport that students are, and should be, the writers and creators of their own educational journeys. However, when it comes to this mantra being a widely adopted practice in public education, there is still much work to be done. The National Education Association (2017), in its article entitled "Identifying Stakeholders' Responsibilities for Closing Achievement Gaps: Stakeholder Actions," recognized students as viable stakeholders, alongside teachers, district, and school leaders, stating that students should "take personal responsibility for their learning; engage with teacher(s), classmates, and others in the school and community; [and] participate, as needed, in supplemental learning programs and opportunities." While engagement with other stakeholders is certainly imperative for students, the One-Minute Meeting process moves students from simply engaging with other stakeholders to pulling a chair up to the table to become equal partners in the educational process known as school. Buchanan et. al (2016), in their highly informed research article based on defining the needs of students with emotional and behavioral disorders, alluded to this need for student feedback by asserting that "prior research has clearly shown that evidence-based programs are more likely to be successfully implemented when stakeholders have the opportunity to provide input on intervention content and delivery. Future research could extend to students themselves and stakeholders in more diverse areas." The One-Minute Meeting places students squarely at the center of processes designed to help them learn and uses their input as the driving force for future implementation.

Shared Vision

Shared vision speaks directly to a leader's ability and tolerance for change, as well as an administrator's leadership capacity within the learning organization. Deal and Peterson (1999) contended that shared visions define what "actions ought to occur; they motivate staff and students by signaling what is important and what will be rewarded; they steer the allocation and distribution of resources, depending on what is considered important or valuable." A shared vision within a learning environment ensures that all stakeholders in a child's education are focused on a central goal or mission and provides the means of achieving that goal. Similarly, Sheppard and Brown (2009) highlighted the centrality of shared visions in professional learning communities by contending, "There is no such thing as a 'learning organization,'[rather, learning organizations refer to a process where constituents] are taking a stand for a vision, for creating a type of organization [they] would truly like to work within and which can thrive in a world of increasing interdependency and change." Within the One-Minute Meeting conceptual framework, shared vision serves to direct the expectations of not only individuals in the learning environment but also the school leaders' carrying out of this vision in the learning community. To shift expectations as well as mindsets in a learning community requires a clear, urgent vision for change. Authentic student-centered processes, such as the One-Minute Meeting, create new paradigms of interdependence and change led by innovative school leaders and their lead teams. Senge (1990) affirmed this notion when he relayed that "you cannot have a learning organization without a shared vision." A shared vision in a learning community presents a credible, yet realistic, picture of the organization that inspires the students, teacher leaders, and school leaders to work collaboratively to reach for the same future goal.

Schools as Learning Communities

Dufour and Eaker (1998) purport that what separates a learning community from an ordinary school is its collective commitment to guiding principles that articulate what the people in the school believe and what they seek to create. Huffman and Hipp (2012) further offered that "these guiding principles are not just articulated by those in positions of leadership; even more important, they are embedded in the hearts and minds of people throughout the school." Student perceptions of their role and experience in a school offer keen insight into how the vision and mission are translated within a learning community. The One-Minute Meeting shines a spotlight on these firsthand experiences and offers clear processes to achieve positive change based on those experiences. School leaders guiding their schools along the fault lines of this shift possess not only an innovative mindset but also a realistic perspective of the stakeholders within their communities. Hiatt-Michael (2001), in her article titled "Schools as Learning Communities: A Vision for Organic School Reform," boldly asserted,

> Educational leaders on the threshold of the new millennium are critically aware that their students and communities do not face the same life as their parents. The demands on society to adapt to globalization have forced all organizations that wish to survive and remain competitive to operate as learning organizations. As educators assess and reflect on the future needs of education, educational leaders are repeatedly discussing the merits of schools as learning organizations. (p. 114)

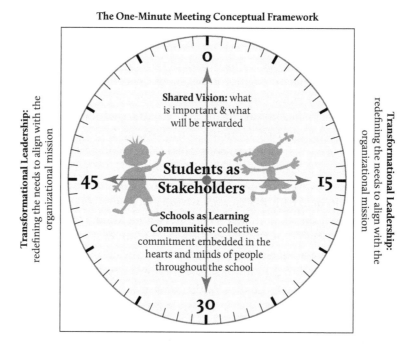

FIGURE 4.1 This conceptual framework helps school leaders & their teams visualize the critical components of the One-Minute Meeting process as it relates to creating student stakeholders in their school.

The 21st Century Is Here

School leaders leading our nation's schools must cease discussing, analyzing, and projecting the 21st century as if it is coming. Alas, at almost 2 decades into this whirlwind of an era, it is clear that the students entering schools each day are changing at an alarming rate. With the advances in instructional technology, smart devices, and social media, the youth of America are a very different concoction of influences than the simple elixirs of the 20th century. No longer do third graders who have never been to the zoo read about lions and tigers and bears in their science textbooks. Rather, they have only to place their cardboard Google glasses on their faces, and with a quick download on a smart device, they are immediately transported to the San Diego Zoo right outside the tiger exhibit! Pig and frog dissections have been replaced with laser-like simulations broadcasted from across the globe, and the beloved pen pal exercises have been replaced with live Skype or Google Hangout sessions with students and teachers in India, China, and Australia. The 21st century is here, and it is not slowing down.

For centuries, the archetypal school was a silent microcosm of teachers instructing whole groups of students who at predetermined times were allowed to raise their hands and give automated, automatic answers that barely scraped the surface of deeper understanding. No thought was given to individuals' learning needs; students' personal skills and talents were not considered, nor were teachers praised for their ability to enhance the curriculum or the learning community with their leadership abilities. Covey (2005) stated that when "people see people and not behaviors, they use that mirror to reflect the best in them." What if all school leaders looked through that mirror to magnify the best in the students and in turn shone that same mirror on the guiding policies, instructional frameworks, and pedagogies affecting teaching and learning? Educators would maximize their potential to educate, and students would maximize their ability to not only learn but also succeed. Phrases such as "he just fell through the cracks," "she will never amount to anything," and "we need to just get him tested" would cease to exist. It starts with changing these habits as a body of professionals.

Covey (2005) was a loyal advocate for a new type of education, professing, "A new reality has emerged, a new economy, a new challenge." In his book, *The 8th Habit: From Effectiveness to Greatness*, Covey presented a construct that lies at the heart of 21st-century education for 21st-century students with 21st-century leaders at the helm. To effect positive change and transform schools into collaborative, influential models of excellence, school leaders must examine themselves and change processes and mindsets that have been ingrained in the general populace since birth. Changing habits is perhaps the most daunting, yet enlightening, reality in the human existence. Humans develop many habits from a young age and tend to maintain these behaviors throughout the course of their lifetimes. Schools have adopted and legalized habits that unlike other industries remained obsolete and ineffective despite the changes in economy, lifestyles, technology, etc., and now public education is witnessing one of the greatest revolutions as the old and the new clash to make way for a type of school and education that can be led only by leaders who fully embrace and manifest the eighth habit.

School leaders must be incredibly people savvy to begin cultivating new habits within their schools. Education is a people business, and innovative school leaders fully understand that the process involves little people and big people working together to learn and grow from each other on a daily basis. The One-Minute Meeting places students in the center of this daily interaction to drive the learning community in the direction of where the 21st century is forcing schools at light-year speed. Perhaps the most piercing call to combat is Covey's definition of leadership: "Leadership is communicating to people their worth and potential so clearly that they come to see it in themselves." That mirror that was used to help the learning community see the good in others must be implanted in each stakeholder's heart, mind, and soul to help them see the good within themselves, particularly our students—and the accomplishment of this task means the difference between an emerging knowledge leader and a courageous one.

With the advancements in technology comes the ongoing war between educators and the technology that is slowly or quickly (depending on district leadership, fiscal resources, and access to devices) replacing traditional instruction. Some veteran teacher leaders scoff at the one-to-world initiatives sweeping the country, citing technology as "the reason these students do not know how to spell, think critically, or have a decent conversation." Meanwhile, some beginning teacher leaders and those embracing the technology craze celebrate the new phenomenon, claiming that technology "disintegrates the barriers between the students and learning." The valiant voice that rarely chimes into this argument is the consumer of the required professional development for instructional technology, the user of the new district-adopted learning management system, and the firsthand observer of the lesson plans created to increase substitution, augmentation, modification, and redefinition. The One-Minute Meeting raises the volume on students' voices and makes them the lead singers in the transformation process. The process itself provides every child in the school with an opportunity that will serve to inspire their relationship with learning. Dewey (1916) believed the process is about creating that one unique opportunity for one child wherein they see themselves as successful, and they want to relive that feeling again. Particularly for students in low socioeconomic settings, students who will go on to be first-generation college attendees, or students who sincerely want a stake in their own future, the One-Minute Meeting provides a spotlight for them to design their education their way and provide purposeful feedback on current practices.

Dewey (1916) conveyed in his most acclaimed work, *Democracy and Education*, that "processes of instruction are unified in the degree in which they center in the production of good habits of thinking." To foster a community of successful thinkers and problem solvers, a school leader needs commitment, foresight, and purpose. By using the foresight of where leaders want their students to end up and what they want them to become, the One-Minute Meeting serves to define the process as well. Courageous school leaders in the 21st century know that it takes an entire learning community for a child to be successful. While commitment, foresight, and purpose will not guarantee academic achievement and success for every child in the school, it will ensure that at least huge strides have been made in the right direction.

One-Minute Challenge:

Take 1 minute to reflect deeply on the role students play in your school. As an innovative school leader, elevating students as stakeholders is a necessary step toward transformation. Are the students encouraged to have a voice both in and outside the classroom about their experiences in your building? Where are the outlets for students to express themselves and provide feedback to other stakeholders about the celebrations and challenges they are facing? What might students say about your school if given the opportunity to write a news article like Braxley's? Share your reflections with key decision makers in your school and begin discussing the next steps.

One-Minute Post-Pandemic Strategy

Students express themselves in a myriad of modalities including song, dance, spoken word, music, and more. After living through and having their educational journey disrupted by COVID-19, some students might have difficulty expressing themselves verbally. As a team, work closely with mental health professionals, school counselors, and support staff in your school community to brainstorm opportunities for students to express how they may be feeling post-pandemic. Creating safe, confidential, and free spaces for students to process their thoughts and feelings pre- and post-pandemic provides another avenue for school leaders to respond to students' needs.

Image Credits

5

Students as Evaluators

One-Minute Reflection Question:
How can students' formal and informal evaluations of teaching serve to inform the current state of learning in a school?

In this chapter, school leaders will shift their evaluative lenses to offer students the opportunity to provide feedback on teaching and learning in their schools. For centuries, school leaders and administrators have engaged in the process of providing formal and informal feedback to teacher leaders, support staff, and district leaders. From fully scripted classroom observations with a focus on content standards to calibrated instructional walk-throughs with district personnel, school leaders have long held onto the reins of feedback and improvement in the construct of public education. Providing students with the training necessary to articulate themselves is a critical step in the One-Minute Meeting process, as it allows students to express themselves accurately and descriptively. Creating a learning community centered on student achievement starts with helping students to communicate about their own educational journey.

I am not learning a whole lot in this class.
—A truthful but hopeful fourth grader

In many ways, FT Elementary was thriving. The ongoing Facebook banter in our small community had shifted from the long-standing complaints and negative feedback to the small but significant changes that were taking place schoolwide and in classrooms. Even the Walmart© conversation was buzzing around what was happening at FT Elementary, due in large part to our team's intentional training and conversations in every informal gathering. We made sure that our teacher leaders and support staff were aware that the best marketing for any school starts with the people who learn and work there. If we wanted to transform our culture, it would begin internally. FT Elementary's lead team worked closely with SIT to tackle issues and problems collectively.

We even conducted a role play during a faculty meeting, which involved our faculty and staff practicing possible responses to the negativity they might face in the community. Empowering our teacher leaders with the language to express themselves helped them navigate their own professional experience rather than expending energy to defend it.

There was still much work to be done instructionally in our school. At 32% proficient based on our state's mandated EOG assessments, we knew that rebuilding the instructional framework would be a focus for the team, along with bolstering the morale needed to sustain it. ILT spent a lot of time discussing the quality of instruction being rendered to our students. We were fortunate to have some teachers whose instruction was absolutely stellar. Their genuine love for children and their craft shone in every aspect of teaching and learning in their classrooms. From lesson planning and classroom management to differentiation of instruction to family engagement, these distinguished teacher leaders were model educators who kept students first in every way. And then there were the other teacher leaders—the ones our team members debated about at length in terms of poor instructional implementation, lack of classroom management, and whether their hearts and minds were focused on FT Elementary's mission at all. These were the classrooms where our team strategically spent the most time.

I walked into Mrs. Wolfe's fourth-grade classroom for the second time in a week. Our team had created a coaching plan for her that consisted of an intense focus on improving classroom management and increasing student engagement. So far, the plan had only been partially embraced by Mrs. Wolfe, and earlier observations and walk-throughs provided evidence that students were struggling in her classroom. There was a lot going on during this particular science lesson, including three students in the corner of the room working on their Chromebooks, several students sprawled on the floor working in pairs, and other individual students sitting at their desks all working on different assignments. Mrs. Wolfe stood at the front of the room lecturing to three students who were taking notes with notepads and pencils. On the board, she had scribbled a few vocabulary words, including *habitat*, *jungle*, *ocean*, and *ecosystem*, and there was an assignment on the board that instructed students to read their short articles on ecosystems and answer the questions in their interactive science notebooks. I observed for several minutes, noticing that one student was falling asleep at his Chromebook before his fellow classmate quietly nudged him awake. His eyes locked with mine, and I indiscreetly motioned for him to sit up and get back to work. Mrs. Wolfe, finally realizing that I was conducting a formal observation, switched gears with her lecture and directed the class to wrap up their activities and join her on the carpet. As the students were transitioning, I made my way over to a student who had been sitting quietly at her desk reading since I entered the room. I noticed that she had a library book in her hands that appeared to be well above fourth-grade level. I asked her what she was reading, and she replied, "This is a book on biomes. I love reading about nature, and this particular book is about the taiga. Did you know that the taiga is the world's largest biome apart from the oceans?"

Impressed and proud, I responded, "No, I certainly did not know that. Wow! Did you learn all that from Mrs. Wolfe?" There was a flicker in this sharp-witted fourth grader's eyes, and she immediately looked away. "What is it dear? What's wrong?" I asked, placing my hand on her shoulder to comfort her.

Almost all of her classmates had gathered on the carpet at this point, and I motioned for her to join them when all of a sudden, she timidly moved close to my ear and whispered, "I am not learning a whole lot in this class. I read on my own." As she quickly made her way to her spot on the carpet, a deep sadness overtook me. This truthful but yet hopeful fourth grader had issued a call to action to the leaders at FT Elementary, and we needed to answer. Urgently.

Creating Opportunities for Feedback

Throughout the disaggregated context of a school day, there are a plethora of traditional processes that occur in schools across the nation on a daily basis. From arrival and dismissal, hall duty and cafeteria duty, morning work and pop quizzes, to field trips and small group assignments, the manner in which America does school has not drastically changed over the past 150 years. Within this calculated and predictable schedule, there exist multiple opportunities for stakeholders to provide feedback. While the bulk of formal training and professional development for school leaders has historically focused on formal and informal observation of instructional implementation by teacher leaders, the One-Minute Meeting process seeks to shift the focus to the students themselves. Student stakeholders possess a bird's-eye view of the school day from start to finish. They are the listeners of the directions given at the beginning of every class assignment, the bus riders each morning and afternoon, the victims of pop quizzes given without warning, and the colleagues to classmates they may or may not have chosen. Student stakeholders are a powerful voice and source of information in each and every school in the country.

Unfortunately, student stakeholders are rarely tapped for their keen insight and perspective on the goings-on within a school. According to Shafer (2017), "The benefits of student feedback are deep and wide—but not always recognized." With public education having such a long-standing history of research-based practice and pedagogy, it would seem that the benefit of using student stakeholders would be a popular transformative strategy in the 21st century. The process for effectively implementing such a practice, however, can look different within the context of each school. The One-Minute Meeting allows school leaders to take this journey with respect to the idiosyncrasies that make their student demographics, school dynamics, and learning communities unique. This is particularly critical when school leaders consider the rapid change of our society and its effect on student demographics. Each school year brings new challenges with students, including access and influence of social media, increasing mental health concerns, and pedagogical approaches to using instructional technology with 21st-century learners. The idea of school is changing, and innovative school leaders and their teams must create opportunities for learning communities to transform along with it. According to Bragg and Fielding (2003), who conducted extensive studies on students as researchers,

> One key arena for participation should be schools, where in recent years young people have come under increasing pressure: they often feel that they are subject to an ever-greater workload and burden of testing, their performance is heavily scrutinised, and even their achievements are often dismissed as evidence of falling standards. Yet research suggests that, in practice, schools still provide

disappointingly few opportunities for students to express their views and contribute meaningfully to shaping school life (Alderson and Arnold, 1999; Wyse, 2001). This situation contrasts with the world beyond the school, where young people have increasing economic power, social maturity, funds of informal knowledge derived from the rich leisure media culture surrounding them, and a greater sense of entitlement. If they fail to engage their students, schools will miss out on valuable opportunities to develop young people's skills, improve provision, and promote citizenship and social inclusion.

For far too long, school has not mirrored the world that it claims to prepare students for. John Dewey, a true educational philosopher who understood the complexities of the changing world and its implications on public education, posed 21st-century challenges at the beginning of the 20th century. In terms of preparing young people for occupations that have yet to be invented, Dewey (1915) stated, "Yet there is a real problem: how shall we retain these advantages, and yet introduce into the school something representing the other side of life—occupations which exact personal responsibilities and which train the child in relation to the physical realities of life?" Educators and school leaders are charged with the amazing task of directing the learning of a single student to develop a society that imparts meaningful knowledge unto future generations of young learners. As educators, bringing together a multitude of students to create a microcosm of educated individuals who will be contributing citizens to the larger community and, ultimately, the world is a daunting task. Perhaps even more enormous a task than that of preparing students for society is guiding these students toward recognizing the significance in their life's work. Dewey (1915) went on to suggest that "the great thing for one as for the other is that each shall have had the education which enables [the student] to see within his daily work all there is in it of large and human significance." Innovative school leaders creating systems of change around student feedback promote the importance of every student's daily work as significant to the success of the learning community.

If schools want to ensure that students enroll, enlist, or become employed after their K–12 education, then there must be processes in place that boldly promote their voices, their perspectives, and their needs as vital at the table. There is not one Fortune 500 company in business today that does not engage in strategic research, marketing, and training to better understand how they can constantly improve services and products for their customers. From surveys, to focus groups and incentives, to social media, these companies are consistently seeking the customer voice to help guide them to provide an excellent experience every time. Why, then, are American schools that serve almost 57 million students each day not tapping their number-one customer for feedback on improving public education? It is time to create opportunities for students to be heard.

Teaching Evaluative Language to Students

Gleaning feedback creates powerful relationships that require intentional communication on a central idea. The One-Minute Meeting process focuses on creating conditions for optimal teaching and learning for students within the context of the schools they currently attend. As experts of their own experiences, students possess a vivid and, often-times, strikingly candid perspective that can shed light on opportunities for improvement within the learning community. Shafer (2017) asserted, "When schools create a culture of feedback, they 'send a strong signal to students that they care about their point of view, while also creating opportunities to model how to productively receive and respond to feedback.'" To ensure that students are able to effectively express themselves, school leaders and their teams must develop procedures for teaching evaluative language to students. The One-Minute Meeting process asks students to think critically about their day-to-day experiences and articulate these experiences to adults. Students in public schools possess a wide range of backgrounds, ethnicities, cultures, and creeds that have all largely influenced the experiences they have in this world. Academic research confirms that students from poorer socioeconomic backgrounds are inherently at a disadvantage when compared to their more affluent classmates. In terms of exposure to cultural experiences, the acquisition of vocabulary, and the importance of education as a whole, students from poorer backgrounds enter into school disadvantaged from day one. Not only is the situation difficult and challenging but also there are elements that are beyond the realm of school control, including living conditions, cultural dif-ferences, and, oftentimes, economic hardships that may or may not prevent students from learning at their best.

School leaders who recognize these disadvantages and widening language gaps are better able to implement the One-Minute Meeting process by ensuring that students are exposed to vocabulary that helps them accurately describe their experiences. Paulo Freire (1998), in his highly acclaimed work *Teachers as Cultural Workers: Letters to Those Who Dare Teach*, offers a refreshing and astounding outlook to individuals of American society and the outlook of the national make-up as a whole. As 21st-century thinkers and learners, Americans are dealing with a world that is changing at an alarming rate. Diversity, language, values, and, ultimately, culture are undergoing a great transforma-tion, which deepens their implications on education as it stands today. For students and the adults who teach them to become more culturally competent, people must become what Freire refers to as literate: "When men and women realize that they themselves are the makers of culture, they have accomplished, or nearly accomplished, the first step toward feeling the importance, the necessity, and the possibility of owning reading and writing. They become literate, politically speaking." When students are afforded the opportunity to know, understand, and familiarize themselves with this rich vocab-ulary, then the ultimate goals of developing culture commence. Teacher leaders and school leaders embarking on the One-Minute Meeting process must understand that the restriction of expression or instruction also limits the nurturing of literacy in a society. How can public educators, as thinkers and learners, limit students' access to creativity, questions, or pedagogy when everyone brings a different outlook and local language to the concepts and issues within schools? Developing students who are truly literate positions a level of power within students' reach that they have historically not had access to.

Whether one is a school leader in elementary, middle, or high school, evaluative language can open a student's expression in a multitude of ways. Beginning with the instructional benefits, school leaders and their ILTs can start the process of infusing evaluative language into their schools with schoolwide literacy initiatives. Writing is an influential, instructional strategy that places the power of language in the hands of students. Kindergarten teams, for example, could start with foundational vocabulary, such as *good* and *bad*. School leaders and ILTs would then work with the kindergarten teachers to create interactive lessons and modules that teach students to use new words other than *good* and *bad* appropriately. High school students could start with writing first-draft cover letters or admissions essays describing their high school experiences. The team would then guide the English department and the school's guidance counselors in working closely with the high schoolers through the writing process to increase their use of evaluative language. Brunch et al. (2017) addressed the need for collaborative decision making with initiatives of this nature by stating, "Teacher teams can collaborate and use the same prompts or assignments across grades or disciplines to assess overall strengths and areas of improvement. By sharing assessment data on students, teachers gain a stronger sense of student ability and minimize the number of assessments needed in a single discipline or grade."

School leaders will also lead teams to think strategically about how students can authentically use their new vocabulary in authentic learning situations: Provide students with opportunities in the classroom to offer feedback on lessons using their new vocabulary. Choose a student from each grade level to share a new evaluative word of the day during the morning announcements. Display student exemplars in the hallway to provide other students with opportunities to read their classmates' work. Allowing students to engage in initiatives that are directly tied to the school's mission has a great effect on culture. By allowing the lead instructional team to work closely with SIT and teacher leaders to develop these initiatives, school leaders will begin to observe shifts in the manner in which students are describing their surroundings, responding to instruction, and communicating with others.

Student Surveys

It would seem to be a rather obvious course of action to simply ask students to provide their thoughts on teaching and learning, particularly if one was seeking ways to improve the school overall. Gleaning this type of feedback, however, comes fraught with a plethora of side effects, including the most daunting of them all: the truth. What if teaching and learning in a school are ineffective? What if students are bored out of their minds in a classroom that is seemingly engaging and pedagogically sound? And what if that feedback was received by teacher leaders, support staff, and school leaders? A shift in the right direction might occur! Addressing sheer humanity in the process of gleaning feedback is one of the most critical responsibilities of a school leader when implementing the One-Minute Meeting process. There will be comments made regarding teaching and learning that will be uncomfortable to accept but imagine how uncomfortable it has been for the students to live through it day after day. There will be opportunities for discussion and analysis that have never been explored among SITs but imagine the depth to which schools will urgently transform their practices by engaging in these discussions. Earp (2018) pointed out the benefits of these uncomfortable, but crucial, conversations by stating, "There are some uncomfortable learnings at times when our students are really honest but if the relationships are there then both the relationships and the learning environment become stronger and more transparent. The sense that learning is something we do together is motivating for students as well as for teachers."

Student surveys offer students a means to communicate their thoughts and feelings, which creates connections between the learner and the learning in a school. Much like the introduction of evaluative language within a school setting, surveys can be delivered in a variety of ways from online to paper and pencil or formal interview to informal group settings. Depending on the instructional level of students, picture surveys or translated surveys can also be developed for students with exceptionalities or students with language barriers. Choosing an area of focus should be the task of SIT and ILT. Determine what areas of teaching and learning need to be addressed. Perhaps ELA scores have been trending negatively or maybe the new math program presents challenges for the teacher leaders and learners in the building. Focusing on a specific area allows students to concentrate their responses specifically to areas that require improvement. Edutopia (2016) highlighted the importance of student surveys in an article entitled "Improving Teaching With Expert Feedback—From Students," which offers school leaders tips for implementation, including the need to "take your time with introducing student surveys to your staff before having them implement them. Lombardi familiarized her faculty with student surveys over a number of meetings before they actually started using them. All staff went through a trial run of having their students take the surveys." The more comfortable educational teams are with the process of introducing, gleaning, and disaggregating the results of student surveys, the more effective student feedback will be in the building overall.

School leaders committed to the journey of transformation within a school are deeply entrenched in the work from the ground up. While ILTs and SITs are pivotal to clarifying the mission and making it happen on a daily basis, the school leader truly sets the tone for the type of transformation that occurs and how quickly that transformation begins to take root. Earp (2018) argued, "With a school-wide approach we suggest that it is really important that senior leadership are seen to be part of this process [...] and above all be open with students about what you are doing and why—they too need to take it seriously and see it is making a positive difference or they will do it in a way that is superficial and not very useful." Transformational leaders do not simply lead the charge for change—they bring others along with them. Oftentimes, school leaders are guilty of igniting the flame for massive revolution but leave those on the battlefield wondering why they are fighting in the first place. Be intentional about explaining why students' voices and perspectives are critical to change, and this will create an atmosphere of success for all.

Student surveys can also help school leaders and their lead teams begin rewriting the narrative for failing public schools. Ever since the 1950s, when television broadcasts became the primary mode of communication for our nation, the media has portrayed education in a negative light that has directly affected the perception of education as it exists today. According to Pepin (2007), "Media representations tend to reinforce public perceptions concerning the causes of school failure as attributable primarily to failing teachers and/or school structures rather than contextual factors such as generational poverty or culturally biased tests." In this era of high-stakes testing, the media has done a phenomenal job of turning the tables on schools', teachers', and students' performances, claiming that teachers are not adequately preparing students for productive lives as citizens or successful careers. The media has gone even further to allude to the mental, as well as emotional, effects of high-stakes testing on our students and the lack of resources available to address each student's needs adequately and appropriately. The public then feeds into this media frenzy, heightening the stress levels of students and educators alike. School leaders using the One-Minute Meeting process will learn to celebrate small wins. Using the feedback and data gained from student surveys and one-on-one conversations will shed light on positive moments and effective practices happening throughout the building. Considering the implications media has in the 21st century on classrooms and the general public's outlook on public education, seeking a balance between the truth and reality can be obtained by turning the volume up on what the students have to say.

One-Minute Challenge:
Gather your team of instructional evaluators at your school. This will include your assistant principals, instructional facilitators, and content leads (if applicable). Ask each team member to take 1 minute and write down areas in the school where there is no evidence of learning. Remind the evaluative team that this information is to be kept confidential but that identifying the weak areas is necessary to begin identifying weak instructional areas in the building that are keeping students from being successful. Share your lists as a team, determine commonalities among the responses, and begin gleaning instructional data and evidence to determine the next steps.

One-Minute Post-Pandemic Strategy
The abrupt halt to the 2019-2020 school year in mid-March has exacerbated the already massive academic gaps that existed for students in core content areas. As schools work to redesign teaching and learning, utilize student surveys as an optimal method for collecting student feedback on how they perceive these learning gaps and the most effective way to address them.

6

Students as Change Agents

One-Minute Reflection Question:
How can school leaders work to shift positional power to student stakeholders to maximize their perspectives and perceptions of "school?"

In this chapter, school leaders will literally and figuratively position their lead instructional teams to glean a new perspective of leadership from the vantage point of their students. There is an adage that calls for children, particularly of a young age, to "do as I say and not as I do." In working to transform school environments, school leaders must be aware that student stakeholders are not only keenly observant of the words of the adults in the building but also more astutely aware of their actions. As teacher leaders, support staff, and community stakeholders move throughout the building busy with the activities and events of the school day, students notice each and every interaction, nuance, and communication that takes place. As they build their own opinions of school over the course of a potentially 13-year career, there is a wealth of information and feedback that they can offer on the process of school improvement. The One-Minute Meeting process builds a bridge between student stakeholders and the educational leaders who support them all while building a platform on which both groups can stand to survey the school landscape hand in hand.

> *Dr. Hemphill, you sit there. I got this!*
> —**Laila, a second grader**

It was not uncommon for our team at FT Elementary to find opportunities for students to lead. Our SIT and ILT had spent many hours discussing the power of leadership in the building and put several initiatives in place to ensure that stakeholders groups had an opportunity to lead from the helm. Teacher leaders, for example, had been given the opportunity to lead professional development workshops from the comfort of their own classrooms during our monthly Techie Tuesdays. Classroom teachers who were using instructional technology effectively were asked by ILT to offer a workshop-style training to their colleagues based on a specific technology tool, strategy, website, or device. The teacher leader then developed the session with the help of the instructional facilitator, and the session was added to the agenda for the upcoming Techie Tuesday. Teachers were given the agenda prior to that month's workshop and were given the freedom to choose their sessions to attend in whole or in part during the allotted time. It was professional development for teacher leaders created by teacher leaders, and the effect on student achievement was significant. Teachers were reaching students across multiple modalities, student engagement was increasing based on data from classroom walk-throughs, and teacher leaders voiced that they actually looked forward to professional development sessions and actively sought out opportunities to lead it!

We were elated at the increase in buy-in, particularly as it related to instructional initiatives at FT Elementary, but our team did not want to stop there. As an ILT, we asked ourselves, "What are some opportunities for *students* to lead in the building that will give them the opportunity to develop real-world skills *and* help our school improve?" The answer came one day during morning announcements in the form of a tiny second-grade student. My assistant principal and I took turns with the morning greetings, and we would regularly choose a couple of students to assist us with the process. From the Pledge of Allegiance, to our school's PBIS creed, to the reading of the lunch menu and daily reminders, there were plenty of opportunities for our students' voices to be heard—literally! This particular day, I had chosen Laila. During a walk-through in her classroom the day before, Laila wowed the class with her summary of a book the class had been reading, and she not only offered a splendid explanation of the theme of the book but also threw in some mini lessons about plot for good measure! I was so proud of her confidence and candor that I asked her if she would assist me the next morning with announcements, to which she happily agreed.

That morning, after Laila and another student tidied up their workspaces in the corner of my office and got ready to join me at the intercom system, Laila looked up at me and said, "Dr. Hemphill, can I be your assistant principal? It looks like you could use some help around here!" Baffled at her request and even more bewildered about the latter part of the appeal, I stifled a chuckle and said, "Well, goodness, Laila! Do you think you're up for the job? It is a lot of work and responsibility." My apparent doubt in her ability to handle the job must have offended our 3-foot learner who responded with a scoff: "Dr. Hemphill, you sit there. I got this!" And she was absolutely right. The next day, after receiving permission from her parents to shadow me for a portion of the instructional day, Laila arrived in the main office dressed to impress. With a beautiful blue dress adorned with sunflowers and her best kitten heels, Laila assisted me in doing classroom walk-throughs, lunch duty, and even responding to emails to parents and guardians. She had insisted on carrying her own clipboard and pen, courtesy of our supply closet, and although my walkie weighed almost as much as she did, she never dropped it or fumbled under its weight as we made our rounds. What surprised me even more, however, was Laila's response to students and staff during our time together. She lovingly but firmly reminded students lined up at the bathroom to stand on the jet decals positioned on the floor. She left me standing in the hallway to go into a classroom and reminded a fourth grader to mind his behavior when she heard him yelling from the hallway, and she even interjected a solid "10-4" in acknowledgment of a call on the radio.

As we wrapped up our time together, I sat down to debrief Laila on the day's events. I asked the petite soon-to-be principal what her thoughts were on her role today and if she made any observations that I could take back to SIT. Her response was brief but insightful as she stated, "It was a good day, and I had a lot of fun being the assistant principal. I wish kids would follow all the rules, but that's why they have you and the teachers to keep them on track. I liked going into other classrooms too. Some of the teachers need some help with their teaching, but they are working hard. When can I be the assistant principal again?" And out of the mouth of our tiniest, but perhaps most powerful, stakeholder it was confirmed that FT Elementary was doing something right.

Addressing the Leadership Gap

Traditional academic research approaches the leadership gap from two vantage points. The first is that leaders lack the skills and competencies necessary to lead their organizations effectively based on their individual needs. This type of leadership gap focuses particularly on a knowledge deficit that ultimately leads to rendering the leader ineffective. The second perspective posits that leaders do not focus on the appropriate issues or skills. The latter leadership gap involves mismanagement and misappropriation of human capital, energy, resources, and valuable time. Both instances cause the leader, team, customers, and stakeholders to stray further and further away from their intended goals and the overall mission of the organization. The One-Minute Meeting process shines a light on a tertiary perspective that proposes that the leaders, in the traditional sense of position and title, are in fact not the true leaders in an organization. This third alternative submits that the consumers or constituents themselves are the true leaders, as they experience our organization in its purest and most authentic form. In terms of the transformational leadership required to better understand our schools and the processes that sustain effective change, the third perspective calls for school leaders to promote students as the very change agents from which one gleans feedback, understanding, and potential solutions for shifting their schools toward a trajectory of success.

Students arrive at school each day with a wealth of knowledge and experiences that should inform the daily operations and decision making in the building. From the most affluent neighborhoods to the poorest of demographics, our students are valuable stakeholders in the educational system who are truly underused and undervalued. According to Leithwood and Riehl (2003), schools should work to amplify the impact and value of students' social capital within the building. These authors further contended that "students bring knowledge and information, values and preferences, and behavioral habits and dispositions to school. Students have acquired these in part from their relationships and interactions with parents, community members, and other persons in their social network, hence they are sometimes known as forms of 'social capital.'" Imagine what schools might look like if they were positioned and organized to meet even the most minute of details brought in the front doors by students. Imagine how instruction might be revolutionized if school leaders abandoned the mere lip service of differentiation and worked to ensure that every teacher leader in classrooms delivered truly differentiated curriculum to each and every child. Imagine how the conversations around teaching and learning might affect students' lives if they were authentically based on the students' prior knowledge, values, preferences, and social networks. Student-centered learning is not a new concept in the world of public education, but student-centered leadership is perhaps the newest and most significant when it comes to inspiring change in the 21st century.

Shifting the paradigm and conversation regarding student-centered leadership may cause some school leaders to pivot on the traditional ideas, systems, and policies that currently govern our public schools. Academic research has only recently abandoned the top-down approach to leadership to embrace the new concept of learning communities. While the very definition of community evokes a sense of fellowship with like-minded individuals who share common attitudes, interests, and goals, the very notion is all-encompassing—leaving not one entity or stakeholder group on the outskirts of its influence. A learning community thrives because each individual within its sphere plays a vital and active part in the overall success of the whole. When it comes to public education, students are vital contributors to and participants in the process. Their social capital alone has the power to inform instruction, inspire innovation, and ignite inquiry. According to Leithwood and Riehl (2003),

> Students' social capital becomes an educational asset when it enables them to fit into school life and successfully perform learning tasks. The value of social capital depends in part on what people in the school choose to count as educationally useful. Knowledge and values generated by the linguistic, racial, religious, or cultural diversity of a student's social network may be ignored or discounted when in fact they hold considerable potential for influencing learning.

Employing the One-Minute Meeting process in schools means that school leaders lead their ILTs and SITs into in-depth, meaningful discussions about what is deemed *educationally useful* in their buildings. Students' social capital is an excellent springboard to determine how instruction should be presented and positioned against the backdrop of teaching and learning. It provides contextual support for behavioral reward systems and discipline policies, and it also solidifies the need for honest and transparent conversations on culturally relevant pedagogy. To position our students as change agents in schools, one must begin not with the end in mind but rather the end user.

An Attitude of Excellence

There is a changing of the guard happening across the educational landscape of school leadership. Not only are educators and pracademics abandoning the tradition of top-down leadership silos, but school leaders are adopting new scholastic ideals and new collaborative strategies, as well as a new air of confidence in the wake of this change. Along with these newly minted personas, school leaders who choose the route of transformational leadership often arrive at their schools with an attitude of excellence. This air of greatness is apparent in leaders' communication at all levels, their ability to envision a future for each of their students, and the implementation of a shared vision for all stakeholders. Navigating through the process of the One-Minute Meeting further confirms an unparalleled commitment to excellence as school leaders use students' social capital, knowledge, and expertise as the genesis for change.

Upon embarking on this process, it is evident that the 21st century has brought with it a set of characteristics that do not easily lend themselves toward an attitude of excellence. In fact, Leithwood and Riehl (2003) accurately capture a depiction of the public education scenery when they stated,

> Educational leaders must guide their schools through the challenges posed by an increasingly complex environment. Curriculum standards, achievement benchmarks, programmatic requirements, and other policy directives from many sources generate complicated and unpredictable requirements for schools. Principals must respond to increasing diversity in student characteristics, including cultural background and immigration status, income disparities, physical and mental disabilities, and variation in learning capacities. They must manage new collaborations with other social agencies that serve children. Rapid developments in technologies for teaching and communication require adjustments in the internal workings of schools. These are just a few of the conditions that make schooling more challenging and leadership more essential.

Leading during these conditions requires school leaders to possess a certain perseverance and determination to develop a shared vision that is truly student-centered. While that vision may look different in each school building, its fabric is intricately woven together with the individuality that each student possesses. For students to be elevated to authentic change agents in the building, it takes a school leader who remains steadfast and committed to the transformational journey from the beginning to the next beginning. Allison (1981) addressed the very essence of the leadership necessary to champion student-centered transformation in his work *Public Schools and Weberian Bureaucracy: A Summary* by asserting, "A principal will likely have a personal understanding of his [or her] school. His [or her] administrative actions will be based on and constrained by this image and depending on the results of his actions, elements of the total image will be confirmed or modified." In other words, a school leader with an attitude of excellence will envision students as change agents and automatically begin to align resources, programs, policies, and procedures to match that mental image. It starts with a vision unapologetically devoted to students' best interests.

While the One-Minute Meeting strategy may seem novel in many respects when juxtaposed against the traditional American approach, there are many lessons that one can glean from the student-centered strides that have been occurring internationally for decades. Finland has been deemed one of the best educational systems in the world due in part to the elevated respect for the teaching profession as a whole and the country's intense focus on and study of the whole child and whole teacher. Understanding one's leadership literacy capacity against the American ideal or expectation is critical when infusing an attitude of excellence into a school building. Leadership literacy begins with an understanding of the people, their history, and their unique ethical tapestry. The American leadership model represents the unique fabric of the aforementioned. A leader must first ascertain where the stakeholders in a school come from—beginning with the students—to understand where they are going. Effective leaders who understand and familiarize themselves with the students' rich vocabulary and history can seamlessly align the One-Minute Meeting process with the ultimate goals of the school.

Going against the grain of tradition in American schools means embracing the idea that our schools should indeed be a reflection of the students who learn, grow, and thrive there. According to Bagshaw (2009), "The reason that we in the field of leadership have not been more circumspect in applying the American model of leadership to other world contexts is an uncomplicated manifestation of scholarly ethnocentrism." Leaders play a multifaceted role in the overall development and maintenance of a school community. Effective leaders are able to empathize not only with the stakeholders within the organization but also with those organizations in which transactions and interactions are occurring. The application of ethnocentrism, or cultural judgment, that is limited to one's own culture, value, and moral systems hinders a school community from fully developing and reaching its goals and mission. To lead effectively on a transformational scale, American leaders should be well versed in the types of leadership models by which neighboring countries and their international educational partners operate. Baghsaw (2009) stated, "In the context of the American model, any attempt at leading requires accreting enough support and agreement from the group for a leader-candidate's vision to be pursued." Leading from the perspective of an attitude of excellence has intended and unintended consequences—the most positive of which includes inspiring others to pursue the vision that students can be and should be critical change agents in schools. Generating this support and agreement calls for grassroots leadership that may alter from the traditional American leadership model to change the culture of leadership on the American forefront. This oxymoronic mission may leave American leaders questioning how such a change should occur, but it will also force individuals leading schools to take a closer look at culture, what it is, how it is created, and what variables either impede or lend itself to change. If the culture does not line up with the needs of the school stakeholders and the overall mission, then a school leader must be forthright in guiding the research, organizational stakeholders, and followers to reach a new echelon of change, acceptance, and empathy that will address this leadership gap. Students hold the key to closing this critical divide.

A Culture of High Expectations

Cultural leadership can provide the most solid foundation for deploying and effectively implementing the One-Minute Meeting process, as it offers great change for the professional learning community overall. For a group of educators to take time and reflect and recognize their own actions and belief systems and their indirect effect on the educational, social, and emotional welfare of the students being taught is a grand opportunity to lead courageously and fiercely into the 21st century. Appealing to the needs of each and every student requires school leaders and teacher leaders "to be held by participants in and observers of their reality and to thus influence their actions and perceptions" (Allison, 1981). Imagine the paradigm shift for historically marginalized students in a traditionally Eurocentric classroom to have educators who focus on their personal histories and culture in the context of the curriculum and through every interaction! Not only would their thinking change but also grade levels could work seamlessly throughout the year to ensure that instruction was intensely differentiated and met the needs of not only minority students but all students in helping them achieve success. The One-Minute Meeting process provides the springboard for such imperative conversations and translates the attitude of excellence into a practical, applicable, flexible culture of high expectations throughout the building.

According to Argyris and Schön (1978) and their theory of organizational environment, an organization is like an organism, each of whose cells contain a particular partial, changing image of itself in relation to the whole. Students, teacher leaders, and school leaders are integral organisms in the public school organization, so the changes brought forth from implementing the One-Minute Meeting process will change practice and thinking for all stakeholders. Teachers will learn to be more sensitive to the needs of their students, which will allow learning to increase on both spectrums. A culture of high expectations leaves no one devoid of the clear expectations for their mindset and behavior, as well as the resources available for helping one achieve those expectations. School leaders who implement the One-Minute Meeting will not only help their schools achieve that culture but also model the specific expectations by leading face-to-face in the trenches with both students and teacher leaders. From the intimate one-on-one time with each and every student to the data disaggregation and analysis of students' responses, the One-Minute Meeting transcends the theory of change agents into a tangible practice that places students in the driver's seat toward success!

It has been said that if nothing changes, nothing changes. School leaders who understand the context of their leadership landscape are able to navigate their lead teams and school stakeholders effectively through the process of transformation to make necessary changes in the overall culture of their schools. The One-Minute Meeting changes the perspective with which school leaders, teacher leaders, and district leaders can approach school improvement, data analysis, differentiation, and even informal assessments, all within 60 seconds of focused, purposeful conversation. While the process itself lasts only a minute, the effect of active listening with the most important stakeholder in a school reaps dividends that last well beyond the span of a traditional school year. Students are the leaders American public education has been waiting for, and it is their innovative, yet innocent, contribution to the process of school improvement and educational reform that will literally revolutionize the manner in which public education is implemented. It takes one decision for a school leader to decide to embark on the path to transform a school, and it will take 1 minute to glean vital information from a student to make that transformation possible.

One-Minute Challenge:

This particular challenge will involve choosing one or two student leaders to serve as your assistant principal to shadow you during a portion of the instructional day. Work with the students' parents/guardians to procure permission for them to be excused from their classes and allow the student to truly act in the role of an administrator in your building. During this time with the student, observe their behaviors and responses to the everyday goings-on in the school environment. Schedule time after the student has fulfilled their duty to allow them to reflect on their experience. Take 1 minute to share their reflections with your ILT and SIT to begin a discussion of how students see and interpret their role as change agents in the building.

One-Minute Post-Pandemic Strategy

COVID-19 caused a ripple effect that reverberated through our society; the pandemic began to normalize virtual and remote learning around the world. As school leaders and districts begin to reimagine teaching and learning, keep in mind those voices that may be silenced due to a lack in connectivity, access to Wi-Fi, or a device that provides them access to learning materials and assignments. Creating access points digitally and face-to-face in order that all students can be heard is critical as schools forge post-pandemic teaching and learning strategies.

PART 3 THE QUESTIONS

How Are You Doing Today?

One-Minute Reflection Question:
How can school leaders begin using the One-Minute
Meeting process to not only empower students with soft
skills but also shift the culture of the entire school?

In this chapter, school leaders will begin learning how the three key questions embedded in the One-Minute Meeting process are designed to maximize the transformational potential within a school. One of the key strategies for school leaders leading this initiative is to ensure that they are modeling the way for all stakeholders in the buildings. The first question of the One-Minute Meeting establishes a platform upon which students, teacher leaders, and school leaders can stand side by side to recognize the human within us all. Shifting culture and morale is one of the most prevalent challenges and barriers to school transformation. By positioning our students in a process that has the power to elevate their voices, their thoughts, and their experiences allows schools to use their responses to make real-time changes to the learning environment and school leaders to evoke transformational shifts with urgency.

I suddenly realized for the first time that educators are human too.
—Dr. Hemphill, in her first year of teaching

Every educator in America has experienced the "morning hallway walk." I know I had my share of it. I first experienced the morning hallway walk during my first year of teaching immediately after college. When I moved into my classroom that summer, everyone had been so helpful. My third-grade team offered to meet me at the school on Saturday morning to unload my truckload of classroom resources and decor. The kindergarten team in the primary building took me to lunch one afternoon to welcome me to the school family, and the main office secretary made sure that I got first dibs on filling my classroom supply orders before all the No. 2 pencils and wide-ruled paper were gone. Perhaps it was the abundant sunshine and good weather, or maybe we were all just operating off of the few short weeks of vacation and rest, but everyone seemed friendly and cordial, to say the least.

It was no secret that the first 2 weeks of school had been an eye-opener for me. I was a first-year teacher who had outfitted my classroom to resemble the quintessential learning environment. My open house for my new students and parents had rendered an overwhelmingly positive response, and I could not wait to dive headfirst into teaching. Of course, there were a few behavior problems that would prove to be challenging as the year progressed, and the cafeteria could not seem to remember any of my students' lunch numbers, so I stood for 20 minutes of my 30-minute lunch reading out my students' IDs every day. Sure, my lesson plan template had received less than stellar feedback from our instructional facilitator the first 2 weeks, and no one could seem to tell me how to get the copier on our hallway to work, but nothing seemed insurmountable to me. I had a positive outlook on teaching and life, and I knew that I had a team of well-meaning educators in the building ready to support me if I failed. Or at least I thought that until one morning in September. It was an early morning about 3 weeks after the first day of school. I parked my car outside the upper-level building, unloaded my belongings, and made my way to my classroom. My room was the last door on the left, so the trek from the parking lot was particularly lengthy, and it seemed even longer that morning. I had my first encounter with Mrs. Hall at the door when I entered the building. She was standing at her door looking particularly upset, and I asked in a bright tone, "Good morning, Mrs. Hall! How are you today?"

"Not at all great," she responded in a flat tone before she stepped even further inside her classroom, signaling the end of our conversation.

In an effort to remain positive, I continued walking down the corridor and could see Mrs. Porter approaching me on the opposite side. "Good morning, Mrs. Porter," I said, hopeful that her day was going better than Mrs. Hall's. Much to my shock and amazement, Mrs. Porter locked eyes with me, continued walking, and did not even fix her mouth to respond. I am sure my jaw must have fallen open a bit, and I stood in the middle of the hallway gathering my thoughts. "I know she heard me," I thought to myself, "how could she just not respond?!"

In an attempt to salvage the remainder of this what seemed to be a never-ending journey to my classroom, I took a few more steps and noticed that our building's custodian, Mr. Welch was removing the trash from the teachers' lounge. Mr. Welch was always in good spirits, and he knew all the secrets: which vending machine always had my Pepsi One, whose class was on deck the following week to wash tables in the cafeteria, and where administration kept the good card stock hidden. Mr. Welch was the picture of positivity and shared his demeanor with everyone he met.

In my last attempt to salvage this morning's hallway walk, I poked my head around the corner of the teachers' lounge and whispered, "Good morning, Mr. Welch! How are you today?" He looked up, saw it was me, and started shaking his head. "What's wrong?!" I said a little louder.

"These darn kids have no home training. I just spent an hour scrubbing crayon shavings off the tiled floor in the science lab. It is a shame how some people leave their mess around here. I would hate to see their houses!"

I left Mr. Welch still ranting about the level of cleanliness that was lacking from society today, and I suddenly realized for the first time that educators are human too.

I had asked three people in a span of less than 5 minutes how they were doing, and the truth of the matter was that no one was doing well that morning. Not one educator I had encountered was ready to stand in front of more than 20 little minds and educate them to be their best selves. Not one support staff member was ready to embrace the almost 500 students who would descend upon the building and inevitably make even more messes that will need to be cleaned up. And not one educator I had spoken to that morning exuded the same hopeful demeanor they had effortlessly displayed not 3 weeks ago before the start of school. If this was the sentiment that the adults were exuding, I felt sorry for the students. I vowed that if I ever became a principal, I would work to ensure that the culture of our school would embrace the humans—big and small—who entered through the front doors each morning. The question, "How are you today?" would be a sounding board to learn more about the experiences that were keeping students, teachers, and the leaders in the building from being their best selves that day. And that is exactly what happened when we implemented the One-Minute Meeting at FT Elementary for the first time. We asked students how they were doing today, we listened to their answers, and then we set in motion the processes to help make those days become better.

Rita F. Pierson—Every Kid Needs a Champion

Students in the 21st century do not have it easy. In fact, with all of the advancements in technology, connectivity, and access to information on the World Wide Web, one would think that our young people would have a much easier time navigating their adolescence than generations past. The unfortunate truth is that the youth of America are exposed to more negativity, feelings of worthlessness, depression, violence, and misconduct than at any other time in American history. According to the Office of Adolescent Health (2019), depression is becoming more and more prevalent among American adolescents, and the U.S. Department of Health and Human Services (2019) confirmed that "female high school students (39 percent) were almost twice as likely as male high school students (21 percent) to report depressive symptoms. In 2013, three in 10 high school students (30 percent) reported symptoms of depression in the past year. Of students diagnosed with a major depressive episode, more than six in 10 did not receive treatment." Not only can depression and untreated mental health issues lead to thoughts of suicide but also depression is simply one of many external factors affecting students today. The Office of Adolescent Health, in its report titled the *Picture of Adolescent Health* (2016), goes on to report the following:

> In 2013, more than one in three high school students (35 percent) reported drinking alcohol in the past month (34 percent for males and 35 percent for females). Binge drinking is the most common form of alcohol abuse among adolescents, although any consumption may be harmful.
>
> In 2013, about one in 13 adolescents ages 12–17 (8 percent) reported having used one or more tobacco products, including cigarettes, chewing tobacco, snuff, cigars, and pipe tobacco during the past month. In 2014, almost one in 15 high school

seniors (7 percent) identified as being a daily smoker, and almost one in seven (14 percent) had smoked at least once in the previous month.

In 2013, almost half of high school students (47 percent) reported they had sexual intercourse (46 percent of females and 48 percent of males).

The statistics are mounting against America's youth attaining success, and if there was ever a time that students in public schools needed a champion, it is now!

Schools are perhaps the most consistent and safe places for students, due in part to the systems, policies, procedures, and resources available to them on a weekly basis. While the 21st century has presented new and challenging variables that compromise the overall equity and availability of school safety and student support, it is school leaders and the adults they directly affect who are accountable for creating cultures of belonging that students so desperately need. Rita Pierson (2013), in her world renown TED Talk entitled, *Every Kid Needs a Champion* points directly to the importance of this accountability when she states, "But one of the things that we never discuss or we rarely discuss is the value and importance of human connection. Relationships. James Comer says that no significant learning can occur without a significant relationship. George Washington Carver says all learning is understanding relationships" (0:58–1:21). There are critical relationships that are created and destroyed on a daily basis in public education. Relationships are created between knowledge and students when they have that first "aha" moment after tackling a difficult concept in class for the first time. Relationships are destroyed between students and teachers when the children are berated by their teachers in front of their classmates for seemingly innocent mistakes. Schools create long-lasting relationships with parents and the community when they value external stakeholders as true partners in the educational process, and these same relationships are dismantled when schools perpetuate habits of dishonesty and superiority. And the greatest disservice that public education does for society is when the relationship between a child and learning is annihilated because of failure to build a relationship in the first place.

Applied science research and the study of social behavior confirm that humans seek connections naturally from birth. Whether it is culturally, linguistically, behaviorally, physically, or spiritually, humans need social connection to establish and settle in their space in the world. For students, that connection can come from a teacher who overlooks that missed homework assignment, a guidance counselor who listens to their traumatic episode without judgment, or the cafeteria worker who sneaks in an extra pork chop or ice cream sandwich with a wink and a smile. Students are people who are continually seeking connections to make sense of the world around them. When they cannot find these connections, it makes it much more difficult to concentrate on language arts and math curricula, standardized tests, and homework assignments. Pierson (2013) further elaborates on the need for human connection in schools in her acclaimed TED Talk when she purports, "You know, kids don't learn from people they don't like" (1:48–1:51). As a school leader seeking transformation for a building inhabited by little and big people, your focus must be on establishing the conditions to build, nurture, and sustain productive relationships. Much like adults who suffer from bad days, bad experiences, and bad energy that can oftentimes be carried unknowingly into the schoolhouse, students carry those same experiences into school in their bookbags, on their shoulders, and, most of the time, on their minds. It is the adults who are tasked with connecting with them to help them find their place, their footing, and the right words to better navigate their educational journeys.

Implementing Question #1

The following implementation guide is designed to assist school leaders and their leadership teams as they execute the One-Minute Meeting in their schools. Each of the three key questions in the process is allotted approximately 20 seconds in which to engage the student in meaningful, straightforward dialogue that serves to inform the school stakeholder on areas that directly affect the student. Within the implementation guide, the school leader will find information pertaining to specific age groups and school settings, growth and developmental caveats that should be considered, and resources and support that will help to differentiate the One-Minute Meeting and increase effectiveness.

One-Minute Meeting Implementation Guide

Question 1: How are you doing today?

Duration: 20–22 seconds

Elementary		Resources and Support
Grades K–2	Children in this age group experience the world through fresh eyes and perspectives based primarily on their increasing sense of independence. School leaders implementing the One-Minute Meeting with students in kindergarten through second grade will need to prep the class as a whole prior to meeting with students individually. School leaders should work alongside teacher leaders to walk the class through the One-Minute Meeting process so they know what to expect and that their input is valuable to the school. This will help to set the stage for the one-on-one conversations.	Pillows or mats to meet with students "on their level" Large crayons or pencils Wide-lined writing paper Drawing paper Picture roster of class for students to reference Smiley face chart (happy, indifferent, sad) for students to point or tap Small rewards (i.e., pencil holders, erasers, stickers, PBIS tickets, etc.)
Grades 3–5	Children in this age group are actively acquiring the language and behaviors to fully express themselves and explain the world around them. School leaders implementing the One-Minute Meeting with students in grades 3 through 5 should understand that peer influence plays a big role in the relationships being formed in their lives. When students are asked how they are, their responses will oftentimes be influenced by social standing, challenges, or acceptance in their peer groups.	Scale cards with corresponding faces from one to 10 for students to rate their level of stress, happiness, etc. Picture roster of class for students to reference Small rewards (i.e., pencil holders, erasers, stickers, PBIS tickets, etc.)

(Continued)

One-Minute Meeting Implementation Guide
Question 1: How are you doing today?
Duration: 20–22 seconds

Secondary

Grades 6–8	Students in grades 6 through 8 are grappling with their keen awareness of what is happening in the world and actively searching for their place and role in it. It is critical that school leaders implementing the One-Minute Meeting with middle schoolers are sensitive to their students' opinions, responses, and stories because they can hold the key to the next steps to take with these students.	It may be beneficial to have the guidance counselor, school psychologist/psychiatrist, or student support team on standby during the One-Minute Meetings in middle school because of the nature of Question #1. If a student alludes to self-harm, violence, feelings of sadness, loneliness, depression, etc., immediate action should be taken to help the student address and alleviate those feelings.
Grades 9–12	Students in grades 9 through 12 are reaching the peak and culmination of physical and hormonal changes that began in early adolescence. These students are also about to embark on cognitive processes and decision making that will affect the beginning of their journeys into the real world. School leaders implementing the One-Minute Meeting with high schoolers can position this process as an opportunity for students to be critical stakeholders in the educational processes that govern their schools.	Consider conducting One-Minute Meetings with high schoolers later in the school day when they are more likely to be alert and less likely to be tardy. Research shows that high schoolers are more attentive and focused later in the school day.

Alternative

| Behavior | The One-Minute Meeting is ideal for students with behavior challenges, as it increases one-on-one attention and provides a platform for open-ended responses. When introducing Question #1 with students in this category, keep in mind that responses may be based solely on their current emotional or behavioral state. The timing of this process may need to be altered or amended if the student is not capable of engaging in the process at that time. | Students' behavior charts or copies of behavior goals

Emotion flashcards or visual cues (i.e., angry, mad, frustrated, sad, scared) for students to point or tap

Setting with a minimum of visual/auditory distractions

Sensory tools to help students concentrate |
| --- | --- | --- |

(Continued)

One-Minute Meeting Implementation Guide
Question 1: How are you doing today?
Duration: 20–22 seconds

Alternative

Exceptional	When working with students with exceptionalities, school leaders must reference individual educational plans (IEPs) to ensure that the child's classification, goals, accommodations, and modifications are considered. The One-Minute Meeting process is broken into short, manageable tasks, making it easily adaptable to meet the needs of exceptional students.	Copies of IEP at a Glance, Section 504 Plan, or differentiated education plan (DEP) with academic and behavior goals for reference Emotion flashcards or visual cues (i.e., angry, mad, frustrated, sad, scared) for students to point or tap Setting with a minimum of visual/auditory distractions
Magnet	Students in magnet programs (i.e., Science Technology Engineering Arts Music or STEAM, arts, music, mathematics, etc.) have identified proclivities in certain academic or extracurricular areas of the curriculum. The One-Minute Meeting lends itself to student expression, particularly with Question #1, in that students can respond in ways that demonstrate mastery of their magnet area (i.e., through song, visual arts, algorithms, etc.) School leaders truly have the space to be creative with this process to fully engage students in their responses.	Access to technology (i.e., Chromebooks, tablets, etc.) for students to capture or share responses Alternative settings (i.e., chorus room, band room, science lab, etc.)

How Are You Doing Today? More Than an Icebreaker

Common courtesy teaches us from an early age that when meeting or reengaging with another individual, it is proper to ask how the person is doing. While this age-old practice may seem like second nature to a majority of the educators in a school, consider the power of this simple, yet often overlooked, question. When one human asks another human to provide an update on how they currently see their existence at that moment, it opens the door to a plethora of intimate conversations, possibilities, and even disruptions that either create or destroy relationships. Someone who is having an amazing day may respond, "I am doing fantastic today! I hope you are too." That type of response has a tendency to inspire or motivate the other person, allowing them to see positivity and gain a fresh perspective. However, an individual who is having a terrible day might share, "It's been a horrible day. Absolutely nothing is going right!" This single response breeds negativity and creates a barrage of follow-up questions to help that individual feel better about their current state. School leaders who focus on the power of human connections and healthy relationships in their schools will find that their students are more open to new ideas, quick to share their thoughts and feelings, and eager to learn new strategies for coping. According to Tassione and Inlay (2014), "Students who love school and have healthy relationships with adults have a strong sense of belonging. They know they matter. When they feel that their teachers like them as individuals, they in turn like their teachers. Because of this relationship, they are cooperative and motivated to work hard." When it comes to implementing the One-Minute Meeting, the first and most important question is, *How are you doing today?* The response sets the stage to learn what students are experiencing, as well as how to improve the school in the process.

To move the One-Minute Meeting process from a simple conversation to actionable research, it is imperative that the school leaders and the leadership teams conducting the process be fully present for each student. The response to Question #1 is an intimate window into the world of a child. Consider the students in schools each day who do not engage in meaningful, loving, and positive conversations in their home environments and are instead forced to endure the perils of domestic violence, impoverished surroundings, or simply family members who choose not to speak to them. When a caring adult at school asks, "How are you doing today?" and is sincerely invested in the response, there is an opportunity for authenticity and transparency that will change that child's life for the better. If one student reaps the benefits of developing a constructive relationship with an adult at school, the entire school improves. Asking a student how they are doing is so much more than just a nice icebreaker. It is the power of intentional dialogue with student stakeholders. It is the potential effect of the One-Minute Meeting on an entire school.

One-Minute Challenge:

Take a 1-minute walk through the school at three different times of the day: before the school day begins, in the middle of the school day, and after the students have left for the day. Ask the educators you meet how they are doing today and take notes on the type of responses you receive. Based on that data, determine which areas need to be addressed, possible next steps, and a time line for creating and sustaining a culture of relationships in the school.

One-Minute Post-Pandemic Strategy

Every child truly does deserve a champion, and—considering how quickly the world can pivot in light of the recent pandemic—school leaders should be intentional about creating communication and mentor loops for students and school stakeholders via regular touchpoints throughout the school year. Work with your ILT or school improvement team to ensure that each child in the school has a mentor assigned to them as an extra layer of support and guidance during these unprecedented times. The more support your school builds around students, the more successful they will be!

8

What Is Your Greatest Celebration or What Are You Most Proud of From the Past 9 Weeks (Quarter/Semester)?

One-Minute Reflection Question:
How can school leaders use students' celebrations and proudest moments to elevate and affirm students' voices and perspectives in the school transformation process?

In this chapter, school leaders transition to the second question of the One-Minute Meeting to glean unparalleled perspective from students on what they deem to be their greatest celebrations or proudest moments from the past 9 weeks/quarter/semester. The process of school transformation is birthed from gaining an understanding from and among all school stakeholders. To develop an authentic student-centered culture in a school, it is critical that the school leaders and their ILT first understand what the students deem worthy of celebration. School culture is an intricate concoction of experiences, expertise, knowledge, values, beliefs, and assumptions. Offering students the opportunity to voice firsthand what makes them the proudest lays the first brick in a solid foundation toward shifting physical resources, professional development, human capital, and much-needed attention in a purposeful direction.

> *I have a new baby sister!*
>
> **—Jordan, a proud new big brother**

The One-Minute Meetings at FT Elementary were proving to be a huge success! This was the second semester that we had implemented the 60-second rounds with our elementary students, and we were able to make significant instructional and procedural changes based on the first semester of feedback. After compiling all of the third-grade responses and juxtaposing their first-quarter reading benchmark scores, many of the students shared that they were proud of their growth over the summer and that they maintained or slightly increased their reading levels. When other third-grade students were asked about their greatest celebrations, they mentioned that they increased a level on their written responses. As the ILT combed through benchmark data and matched students' responses, it was clear that those students who deemed reading to be their proudest or celebratory moment also had an elevated score in the first semester as compared to their last semester in second grade. The findings caused our team to begin asking questions: *What instructional strategies were teacher leaders using to support third-grade students at their individual reading levels? How much emphasis was being placed on reading in the third-grade classrooms with students, and how were third-grade teacher leaders celebrating individual students, as well as encouraging the class as a whole?*

The following semester, our team was intentional in how we celebrated our students in the area of reading. We crafted new morning announcements that included shouting out those students who were making strides in their reading journals, during guided reading groups, or spending extra time dissecting their self-selected reading. Our ILT met with the third-grade teachers and helped them brainstorm a list of nonfood rewards for students who increased their progress monitoring. We included everything from extra technology time, free choice during intramurals, school store coupons, and even allowed every student who increased a level to call their parents and brag about their progress! FT Elementary was being proactive and intentional about celebrating what our students deemed important, and the next semester, we saw even greater gains in the second-semester benchmarks in the third grade. Academically, we were continually challenging ourselves, our teacher leaders, and our students to reflect on processes, procedures, and even policies that governed our instruction. Everything was flowing smoothly until the last semester of the school year.

It was the end of the third quarter, and I had been vigilant about ensuring that teacher leaders, our ILT, parents, and community stakeholders understood that it would be all hands on deck as we began preparations for end-of-year testing. We had analyzed our language arts data, our math data, and even our science data for trends. The team had made instructional adjustments in our PLC meetings and in the vertically aligned pacing guide. We had even unpacked the standards that had the highest percentages on the EOG exams so that teacher leaders and their students were well versed in tackling those specific test items. We entered into the third round of One-Minute Meetings armed and ready to prepare our students to do their best on the EOG tests! I started on the fourth-grade classes early that Friday morning, and I pulled out the first-class roster. With only 20 students in this particular class, I walked into Mrs. Kerley's room and motioned for Jordan to join me in the hallway. Jordan was used to the One-Minute Meeting by now, and he excitedly climbed into the plush desk chair I had wheeled from my office. With his feet dangling off the edge, he readied himself for the first question.

"So, Jordan, how are you today?"

He responded with an energetic, "I am doing great, Dr. Hemphill. It's Friday!"

I smiled to myself, and as I proceeded to the next question, I took out the last-quarter benchmark scores as I normally did to ensure that I helped students celebrate their academic accomplishments. I immediately noticed that Jordan's math benchmark had dropped drastically. He had scored an 89 on his second-quarter math benchmark, and we set a goal together that he would try for a 95 next time. Unfortunately, as I ran my finger across the Excel printout, Jordan's score had dropped to a 56!

I braced myself as I asked, "So, Jordan, what is your greatest celebration or what are you most proud of from the past nine weeks?"

He looked up at me with the biggest smile and brightest eyes and responded, "Dr. Hemphill, I have a new baby sister! She is so sweet and little, and she is all I think about while I'm at school. I help my Mom every day when I get home. She cries a lot, especially at night, and I don't get a lot of sleep, but I love her so much!"

With glistening eyes, I high-fived Jordan on his new role as a big brother and realized that that school transformation meant celebrating *every* moment in our students' lives, not just the academic ones.

Every Student Has a Celebration

Every distinctive group of humans has a culture attached to them that characterizes their environment. Whether it is the work culture in a fast-paced, grassroots organization that has built a culture of transparency and innovation for its employees or the Fortune 500 company that has developed a culture based on consistency and tradition, every group is unique in the way it celebrates, acknowledges, and values its employees. Within the learning community, school leaders and their ILTs must recognize that despite the demographics, socioeconomic status, or academic achievements of their students, there is a school culture that drives what is deemed important and valuable in each school. The One-Minute Meeting process allows school leaders to pull a seat up with students to hear and experience firsthand what students believe are their greatest celebrations and proudest moments, as well as offers them the opportunity to voice those junctures out loud. Understanding what students value in the context of their overall experience in school is paramount to shifting school culture and imperative to creating effective school transformation. According to Farr (2011), educators' knowledge base could be reinforced by investigating the role that celebration plays in building classroom learning communities. Many times, the adult stakeholders in a school celebrate the traditional academic accomplishments of their students in a traditional manner. It is not uncommon for teacher leaders to celebrate students who increase their overall scores on formal assessments, reach new echelons on their behavior goals, or simply advocate for their own learning through presentations, projects, or proposals. For decades, schools have used incentive charts, stickers, school coupons, positive notes home, encouraging phone calls, and classroom or schoolwide celebrations as a means to express to students that their growth is meaningful to the overall learning community.

The One-Minute Meeting process, however, positions students in the driver's seat by simply asking them what they believe to be their greatest celebration or proudest moment in the past 9 weeks/semester/grading period. Kouzes and Posner (1990) purported that the incorporation of celebration is a primary function of leadership in general. They referred to this act as "encouraging the heart" and emphasized the importance of taking the time to recognize contributions and celebrate accomplishments. To fully engage students in the process of school transformation, school leaders must create proverbial connections to the experiences that touch the hearts of the students and subsequently seek ways to celebrate alongside the students in their journeys. Elise Trumbull, coauthor of *Managing Diverse Classrooms: How to Build on Students' Cultural Strengths* (Trumbull & Rothstein-Fisch, 2008), asserted,

> If our goal is to reach all students and have as many students as possible achieve at high levels, then we need to understand where they're coming from, how their families are rearing them, and the kinds of values and approaches to learning and using language that families are using so that at least we understand what kids are coming to school with.

Question #2 provides just such a strategy to achieve that particular goal of seeking an understanding of students' values through their language, and each student, no matter their background, experiences, or beliefs, has something to celebrate. Celebrations come in all shapes and sizes. Whether it is a celebration as grandiose as the addition of a new family member, the returning home of an old family member, or a particular life milestone or as seemingly small as learning to make their bed, button their shirt, or peel an orange, there is no such thing as a student having nothing to celebrate! Each celebration or proudest moment shared by a student offers a glimpse into their life and adds meaning and value not only to the One-Minute Meeting process but also to the school as a whole.

Implementing Question #2

As school leaders and their leadership teams continue to execute the One-Minute Meeting process, Question #2 allows students to truly acknowledge either a major celebration or major moment of which they are the proudest. Regardless of what the student chooses to share, allowing the space and opportunity for the child to pay homage to this celebration elevates their voice and perspective in a mighty way. Question #2 opens the door to a child's heart and mind and allows the school leader, teacher leader, or instructional leader to peek into the world through the student's perspective; however, this question requires preparation. With regard to the specific age groups and school settings, the following implementation guide offers insight into ways to adapt the setting and response to Question #2 based on the developmental, mental, socioemotional, or academic needs of the student.

One-Minute Meeting Implementation Guide

Question 2: What is your greatest celebration, or what are you most proud of from the past 9 weeks (quarter/semester?)

Duration: 20–22 seconds

Elementary		Resources and Support
Grades K–2	Children in kindergarten through second grade place a heavy emphasis on play. Many times, their most celebrated moment is associated with their first understanding of organized sports, learning to share a new toy with a friend, or newfound language skills. School leaders implementing Question #2 with K–2 students should prepare to visually and physically exemplify their excitement as students share their greatest celebrations or proudest moments to increase and confirm their confidence. Using pom-poms, clappers, or moderately loud noisemakers to celebrate with the student will help to build excitement and trust and increase the student's self-awareness and self-confidence in their accomplishments.	Pom-poms, clappers, or noisemakers Small rewards (i.e., pencil holders, erasers, stickers, PBIS tickets, etc.)
Grades 3–5	Third through fifth graders are experiencing their first encounters with increased independence, which naturally may be preceded by frustration and self-doubt. As school leaders pose Question #2, it is critical that students' responses land in a safe space to continue the One-Minute process successfully and further build on students' strengths. School leaders implementing this question with students are in a particularly advantageous position to coach them through any potential internal struggles by highlighting their celebrations or proudest moments as learning lessons. Ensuring that one confirms the celebration or proudest moment with a thumbs up, high five, or fist bump (as appropriate) with the student creates a culture of affirmation from which the student can grow and continue learning.	Thumbs up, high five, fist bump (protocol may vary by school and location) Small rewards (i.e., pencil holders, erasers, stickers, PBIS tickets, etc.)
Secondary		
Grades 6–8	Sixth through eighth grade students are typically well versed in their celebrations or lack thereof, as they are acutely sensitive to their perceived role in the world and others' opinions or responses to it. Helping sixth through eighth graders voice their own celebrations and guiding them to accept life's natural consequences opens up trust, which is necessary for gleaning the most constructive and effective responses from students during the One-Minute Meeting. School leaders who pose Question #2 to middle schoolers must be prepared to step into the students' shoes and proverbially walk with them to truly understand how they see themselves in the world. Authentically recognizing a student's celebration with a thumbs up, high five, or fist bump (as appropriate) or providing them with a tangible school reward acknowledges the student's celebration or proudest moment as valid and further provides affirmation for them internally.	Thumbs up, high five, fist bump (protocol may vary by school and location) Tangible school reward (i.e., PBIS reward, 10 minutes of tech time, free choice social time, intramurals, etc.)

(Continued)

One-Minute Meeting Implementation Guide

Question 2: What is your greatest celebration, or what are you most proud of from the past 9 weeks (quarter/semester?)

Duration: 20–22 seconds

Secondary

Grades 9–12	Ninth through twelfth graders are actively embarking on a critical chapter in their lives that will require them to make decisions regarding their immediate futures as contributing citizens of society. As these students further develop their professional personas, as well as deepen their personalities as young adults, their celebrations and/or proudest moments are often associated with college or job training, talents needed in their chosen future careers, or affinities to study in formal and informal schooling after high school. School leaders should understand that posing Question #2 to students in ninth through 12th grade causes students to attach futuristic implications to their celebrations. From sharing their acceptance letters to college or vocational programs, to the choice to enlist, or to simply making a choice to pursue an internship to for a potential future job, high schoolers sharing their proudest moments has massive significance for the One-Minute Meeting process. School leaders can reinforce those soft skills that are needed in the real world and sought after by employers by reinforcing the student's celebration with a firm handshake, purposeful eye contact, and sincere congratulations. Using the One-Minute Meeting process to confirm and affirm students offers learning opportunities that can last a lifetime!	Handshake with eye contact to reinforce soft skills (protocol may vary by school and location) School guidance counselor (if appropriate)

Alternative

Behavior	For students with behavior accommodations, modifications, or adaptabilities, Question #2 is a prime opportunity to allow students to celebrate their accomplishments and/or strides in achieving their behavior goals. School leaders posing this question to students in this category should prepare accordingly by reviewing students' individual behavior plans/goals prior to beginning the One-Minute Meeting process. This provides a solid foundation on which to confirm and affirm the students when they share their celebrations or proudest moments and allows the school leader to connect that particular accomplishment to something the students have been actively working toward.	Fidgets, alternative seating, therapy balls, and therapy bands Copies of students' individual behavior plans/goals Student incentive sheets from past weeks and/or data on students' behavior from previous grading periods Reward sheets or reward stickers (when applicable)

(Continued)

One-Minute Meeting Implementation Guide

Question 2: What is your greatest celebration, or what are you most proud of from the past 9 weeks (quarter/semester?)

Duration: 20–22 seconds

Alternative

Exceptional	When implementing the One-Minute Meeting with students with exceptionalities, it is critical to adapt Question #2 to meet their individual needs and learning styles. School leaders should be well versed in each student's IEP to differentiate according to their diagnoses. Being able to meet students where they are physically, socially, and academically is also critical to fully allow students to communicate their celebrations or proudest moments. For instance, a student who is selectively mute may communicate through written expressions and, therefore, the school leader would communicate their affirmation of the response in a written format. School leaders are encouraged to work closely with a student's general education and special education teacher leader to accommodate and modify Question #2 so that two-way communication is tailored specifically for each student.	Fidgets, alternative seating, therapy balls, and therapy bands Copies of students' IEPs and/or copies of students' individual 504 plans Student incentive sheets from past weeks and/or formal and informal data on students' academic, social, and physical progress from previous grading periods Reward sheets or reward stickers (when applicable)
Magnet	Students enrolled in magnet programs have a particular focus of study or area of interest that generally surrounds their learning. Question #2 opens up opportunities for students to celebrate their accomplishments or share their proudest moments based on their chosen course of study, growth in a particular academic field, or acquisition of a new skill or talent. School leaders should lean into their school theme, vision, and current reward system to innovate how each student's response is recognized. Modeling affirmation in a unique way demonstrates to students the school leader's commitment to not only their individual contribution but also the program of study.	School leaders and their ILTs can create innovative rewards based on their magnet themes or the students' academic proclivities, including opportunities to perform in a talent show, participate in a quiz bowl, or academic competition.

"I Don't Know" Is Not an Option

Asking students to share their greatest celebrations or proudest moments from the previous 9 weeks/quarter/semester, may leave some students stumped. School leaders and their ILTs that implement the One-Minute Meeting with their student bodies must be prepared for all types of responses and arm themselves with strategies and tools to respond accordingly to students who may find it difficult to come up with what they consider an appropriate response. It is critical that the adult stakeholder facilitating the One-Minute Meeting approach those students with positivity, encouragement, and affirmation while maintaining that "I don't know" as a response is not an option. "I don't know" leaves the student feeling as if there is nothing about their life or school experience to celebrate, which defeats the purpose of Question #2. To combat those sentiments, as well as preserve as much of the student's time as possible, school leaders can use the following redirects to shift the student's thinking and potentially elicit a celebratory response:

1. Think about your favorite subject here at school. Can you think of one thing that you have done well in the past 9 weeks/quarter/semester?

2. I was in your classroom (insert time frame), and I remember you (insert occurrence). Would you consider that a celebration?

3. I bet your (insert family member based on individual student's family dynamic) says they are proud of you all the time. What do they say they are proud of you for?

4. It's okay not to know, but I bet if you think really hard you can come up with something to celebrate!

5. I am going to give you a little more time to think about the past couple of weeks. There has to be a time in which you were super proud of yourself.

Depending on the age level of the student, school leaders can add discussion starters to their One-Minute Meeting tool kit over time; however, the goal is that every student walks away from the 60 seconds having shared at least one celebration or proudest moment. Psychologist Polly Campbell (2015) attested, "Moments of celebration make us pause and be mindful, and that boosts our well-being … when we stop to savor the good stuff, we buffer ourselves against the bad and build resilience—and even mini-celebrations can plump up the positive emotions which make it easier to manage the daily challenges that cause major stress." With so many external and internal factors working against the process of successful school transformation, spending 60 seconds on a student celebration can be a colossal drop in the bucket when it comes to building a positive, transparent, and healthy school culture.

One-Minute Challenge:
At the next school improvement meeting, ask each representative/stakeholder to bring one artifact that demonstrates how they celebrate students. It could be a photo of a class party, a student certificate, an encouraging note written in the student planner, or even the special chair given to the student of the day or month. Each stakeholder will have 1 minute to share how they celebrate students in their classrooms/learning environments. Capture this conversation and then juxtapose the responses from Question #2 after completing a round of One-Minute Meetings with the student body. Do the responses from students and the manner in which they are celebrated at your school align? What are the opportunities to strengthen or augment student perspectives when it comes to celebrating students at your school?

One-Minute Post-Pandemic Strategy
Grading policies and procedures around the country have been disrupted by the abrupt ending of the 2019–2020 school year. School leaders should take the opportunity to encourage their ILT and school improvement teams to think holistically about ways to celebrate and encourage students outside of the traditional grading system. As anecdotal data and observation begins to take a front seat in providing student feedback, consider effective and applicable ways to recognize students for their achievements that appeal more to their socioemotional needs in school.

9

What Challenges or Concerns Are You Experiencing in Your Class(es) or in Our School?

One-Minute Reflection Question:
How can the challenges or concerns that students face every day in schools help school leaders develop urgent and critical decision-making processes that greatly improve student outcomes and school culture?

In this chapter, school leaders wrap up the One-Minute Meeting with perhaps the most important question pertaining to the challenges or concerns students are having in regard to their school experiences. Academic research supports that when students are dealing with distractions, negative experiences, or what is considered to be trauma on a daily basis, there can be a serious effect on their academic, social, and emotional well-being. Providing students with a safe space to offer their insights on these experiences voluntarily opens up immeasurable strides in the school transformation process and allows school leaders and their instructional teams to partner with students to alleviate those challenges or concerns. The One-Minute Meeting process was birthed from the perspective of school through the students' experience. The third and final question of the One-Minute Meeting process serves as the lynchpin in effecting positive change in a school that ultimately results in overt policy changes, monitoring expectations, learning protocols, and professional development opportunities that improve school overall for students.

It's not my teacher. It's Tommy!

—A fed up fifth grader

I had spent the majority of the day on the fifth-grade hallway, and I had to admit that I was slightly frustrated. When we began the One-Minute Meeting process at the beginning of the school year, the students' feedback pointed our instructional leadership team in the direction of big instructional changes in the classroom. Several of the students across grade levels mentioned that there was a lack of excitement in the content areas, and we shared that feedback with our teacher leaders and teaching teams. The result was a candid conversation about teaching assignments and the selection and implementation of instructional strategies that would ignite passion in our students. Several teacher leaders admitted that they struggled with specific content areas because of not being comfortable with the curriculum. Others confessed that they simply did not agree with the manner in which the district was asking them to develop instructional lessons and asked if they could explore more innovative ways to deliver instruction to present during professional learning community meetings. Our students were causing the adult stakeholders at our school to reflect deeply, genuinely, and urgently. It seemed that the veil between the students and the teachers who spent almost 8 hours a day with them had been ripped down, exposing teaching and learning, relationship building, and our school culture for exactly what it was: a work in progress.

The fifth graders who had graced the mobile office that day during the One-Minute Meeting confirmed the classic tradition and perplexity of being too old for elementary school yet not old enough mentally for middle school. Several acknowledged during Question #3 that they were worried about going to middle school. Stories shared by their older sisters and brothers plagued their thoughts about multiple class changes, lockers being located far away from scheduled classes, high expectations from teachers and administration, and, yes, the ability to govern their own transition time with no escort to lunch, the common areas, or the gym. Of particular interest to our ILT and me was the marked drop in report grades across the fifth grade in all subject areas from ELA to mathematics and, yes, even science. We had ramped up our instructional strategy and strengthened our fidelity by attending PLCs; however, the schoolwide data showed fifth-grade scores dipping, and we were concerned.

I had just started with my next-to-last fifth-grade class. I was reorganizing my mobile office desk when Taylor pranced out of her classroom and eloquently plopped down into the rolling leather chair. All the students loved sitting in my office desk chair. Many of them said it made them feel "important," and even some of the kindergartners mentioned that when they sat in it, they felt like the principal! Taylor was no exception. She sprawled out in the chair before haphazardly kicking her legs back and forth to make the chair spin. Without looking up, I anchored the chair with my foot to prevent Taylor and my office chair from taking off down the hallway. I secured Taylor's homeroom rosters and located her report card amid the stack that our data manager had printed for me earlier that morning. Taylor, an A+ student, had received less than stellar grades in her ELA and social studies class this past semester.

I launched into the first question of the One-Minute Meeting with, "Taylor, how are you doing today?"

She responded, "I'm doing all right. How are you, Dr. Hemphill?"

For some reason, after years of working with children, it still did my heart good when students showed a genuine interest and care for the adults in their lives.

"I'm doing all right as well, Taylor," I said with a smile. Without skipping a beat, I moved on to Question #2: "What is your greatest celebration or what are you most proud of from the past nine weeks?"

Taylor scrunched up her face to indicate that she was in deep thought before saying, "Well, I thought I was going to fail math, but Mrs. Davis offered tutoring and that helped a lot. I did bring my grade up to a B, so that's good I think."

"That's actually great, Taylor! I am so proud of you!" I asserted. "So tell me, what challenges or concerns are you experiencing in your class(es) or in our school?"

Without hesitation, Taylor launched into an epiphany moment for both of us: "Well, like I said, I thought I was going to fail math, and I like math, but I was struggling. And I know what you think, Dr. Hemphill. It's not my teacher. It's Tommy! He sits right next to me and talks to me the entire time we are in math class. He never pays attention and then always tries to copy off my paper. I told Mrs. Davis on him one time, and he teased me for the rest of the week even in specials. If you could please just move him, I know I would do better."

I reached out my hand to stop Taylor from twirling in the chair, looked her straight in the eye, and said, "Consider it done."

Bloom Versus Maslow

The 21st century ushered in a focus for educators that centered on the whole child. No longer was academic research merely focused on academic achievements and creating conditions simply for classroom success, but researchers, educational leaders, and curriculum developers all shifted their efforts toward the socioemotional and intrinsic experiences of students. From mental health efforts, to trauma-informed pedagogy and culturally relevant pedagogy, to positive behavior management, education has an intense and purposeful nucleus devoted to the development of healthy, happy, and whole children who evolve hopefully into healthy, happy, and whole adults in society. The One-Minute Meeting is a process that not only recognizes that students have challenges on a day-to-day basis but also creates space for them to speak their truth. Developing the whole child means dealing with the whole truth. Question #3 of the One-Minute Meeting serves to unmask the truth that the student lives with, deals with, or struggles with and shows them the power of partnership when efforts are focused on the problem versus the person.

Perhaps one of the most common adages in public education is that one must take care of the Maslow stuff before one can attend to the Bloom stuff. According to Lasic (2009),

> Now, this isn't rocket science. If a kid is hungry, feels threatened, unsafe, not well, insecure or lacking to satisfy any of those needs towards the bottom, he or she might but is not very likely going to scale the heights of Bloom, no matter what you do or what shining resources you throw at them. But unless we ask and/or observe carefully we might actually miss those signs. We push "Bloom" and so often forget or take "Maslow" for granted. Maslow ain't digital either but digital tools can help, a lot.

It is the intentionality of asking the tough questions that makes the One-Minute Meeting so powerful. When school leaders ask students to reflect on the challenges or concerns, they are experiencing in school and then share, they are recognizing the students' power and place in their own educational journeys. Question #3 shifts the conversation from school as a mandate forced upon the child to a real experience happening along with the child. During the 60-second interaction, school leaders and their instructional teams have, as Lasic (2009) mentioned, the opportunity to ask and observe carefully. Some students will be able to articulate their struggles clearly without hesitation. Other students may have difficulty expressing their experiences because they have never been asked or merely because of a lack of trust. These are the key opportunities to observe for school leaders and their instructional teams. Does the student's demeanor completely shift when responding to Question #3? What was the initial reaction when the student attempted to formulate a response? Based on the answer to Question #3, does the student appear hopeful that the challenge or concern can be resolved? When school leaders ask the right questions, they usually glean the right answers, and students are the keepers of the keys to this knowledge!

The One-Minute Meeting is distinct in that it juxtaposes the traditional classroom walk-through or observation, which asks the school leader to take in the learning environment and the stakeholders in it as a whole and replaces the experience with a one-on-one opportunity to glean real-time data that is highly differentiated. Each student will have their own independent challenges and concerns, oftentimes connected to their Maslow needs of self-actualization: esteem, love/belonging, safety, and/or physiology. The school leader's task is to listen to the student with purpose, connect the student's response with the bigger goals and vision of the school, and help address/resolve the student's challenges with urgency.

Implementing Question #3

The One-Minute Meeting wraps up with a question that opens a personal window into students' experiences with their schools. There are a plethora of interactions that occur each day within the walls of a school from students who arrive each morning having survived the trauma from the night before to students who, unfortunately, are dealing with their own personal and internal struggles. Asking what challenges or concerns students are experiencing in their classes on a daily basis requires being prepared to listen to their responses versus simply hearing their answers. When school leaders listen to and authentically engage with students to assist them with their struggles, they automatically glean a first-person perspective into teaching and learning within the building. Asking the last question in the One-Minute Meeting process is merely the first critical step in establishing relationships that will change the trajectory of student success because it is the follow-up and actions taken by school leaders and their leadership teams that will solidify for students the commitment to their overall well-being. It is never easy to share areas and occurrences where one is weak or experiencing difficulty; however, if school leaders engage students in productive dialogue about their struggles, then, ultimately, problem-solving, transparent citizens are produced for the greater society!

One-Minute Meeting Implementation Guide

Question 3: What challenges or concerns are you experiencing in your class(es) or in our school?

Duration: 20–22 seconds

Elementary		Resources and Support
Grades K–2	Students at this stage of development are primarily engaged in social discovery and beginning to develop problem-solving mechanisms/strategies that match their personalities and needs. School leaders will engage with students with varying levels and degrees of emotional vocabulary, so be prepared to encourage students in grades K–2 to freely expound on and talk about their emotions. Help them to appropriately label emotions connected to the concerns or challenges they share and offer age-appropriate models and anecdotes to help them better understand their own experiences.	Emotion vocabulary cards that provide student-friendly visuals and proper emotion naming (i.e., happy, sad, angry, frustrated, etc.) Age-appropriate literature that features young children with big emotions (i.e., *The Way I Feel* by Janan Cain or *Llama Llama Mad at Mama* by Anna Dewdney)
Grades 3–5	Students in grades 3–5 are beginning to find their own paths and patterns in the world through cooperative games, honing of social norms, and seeking the feeling of belonging in their families and friend groups. Children at this age may experience being ostracized for the first time or discouraged by their lack of understanding when it comes to social rules and games. It is critical that school leaders acknowledge these feelings and help students develop effective coping strategies, particularly concerning losing, belonging, and appreciating their own unique personalities.	Peer mentoring can be a powerful resource for students in grades 3–5. Pairing students across grade levels who are experiencing similar challenges can open up needed dialogue and establish student relationships that help to grow the culture of the school. Ensure that students are monitored by a trained and trusted adult leader in the building at all times. Emotion vocabulary cards that provide student-friendly visuals and proper emotion naming (i.e., happy, sad, angry, frustrated, etc.)

(Continued)

One-Minute Meeting Implementation Guide

Question 3: What challenges or concerns are you experiencing in your class(es) or in our school?

Duration: 20–22 seconds

Secondary

Grades 6–8 | Students at this stage of development are eager to be independent of adults, and they experience wavering levels of self-confidence. School leaders working alongside middle schoolers must be aware that children in grades 6–8 are deeply invested in being accepted by their peers and oftentimes struggle with decisions about conforming to peer expectations. As students seek their place of belonging, they may experience internal challenges and external concerns that lend themselves to dramatic effects on their academic well-being. It is critical that students in this age group are surrounded by adults they trust to hear their feelings and that follow-up is swift.

Intramurals are an excellent way to provide students in grades 6–8 with the opportunity to hone their interests and physical skills through voluntary participation. Create a survey to determine sports/activities that students are interested in and then allow multiple opportunities for students to participate.

Genius Hour is another impactful opportunity for students to explore their interests and further develop social/peer skills. Having a wide assortment of offerings requires teacher leaders, school leaders, and community leaders to work together, but it also offers students options that increase involvement, participation, and engagement in the learning environment.

Grades 9–12 | Students in grades 9–12 experience a menagerie of emotional, social, and academic influxes as they navigate their paths into the real world at the end of high school. Oftentimes, mood swings and irritability, as well as regulation of hormones after experiencing puberty and increased pressures at school with sports and extracurricular activities greatly affect students' challenges at school. School leaders should be prepared to hear challenges and concerns centered on teens' impending college and/or career pathways, need for independence from family units, mental health issues, and struggles with developing future aspirations in the face of financial realities (i.e., scholarships, grants, loans, first-generation college, enlisting, etc.).

It is imperative to have a well-trained, knowledgeable guidance department working with students in grades 9–12. From the onset of high school, students should be armed with as much information about their futures as possible, including financial aid, access to resources, and guest speakers/panelists/keynotes who highlight multiple pathways to enrollment, employment, or enlisting after high school. Opportunities to engage in real-world discussions help to alleviate challenges and concerns as students in this age group navigate their way toward graduation.

(Continued)

One-Minute Meeting Implementation Guide

Question 3: What challenges or concerns are you experiencing in your class(es) or in our school?

Duration: 20–22 seconds

Alternative

Behavior	For students with behavior diagnoses or behavior issues, it is not uncommon for them to have adverse coping mechanisms because of their experiences in school. Some students may have dealt with their behaviors since the onset of their school careers while others are newly diagnosed. Regardless of when students began experiencing behavior complications, school leaders should rally around these students to listen intently and help them find their unique pathways to success. Challenges and concerns shared by students with severe-to-mild behaviors should be handled by a knowledgeable team of educators and experts as quickly as possible so as not to derail or distract the student or other students.	There are a plethora of behavior management resources and environmental interventions for students struggling with behavior concerns. School leaders should work closely with teacher leaders and the ILT to procure appropriate professional development for the implementation of positive classroom management (PBIS) decision-making strategies for students, conflict resolution interventions, and even schoolwide incentives for positive behavior.
Exceptional	Students with exceptionalities on either end of the spectrum experience challenges and have legitimate concerns about their school experience. School leaders and their instructional teams must be equipped to respond to students as they share their challenges or concerns, particularly those connected to them reaching their IEP (individualized education plan) or DEP goals.	Copies of IEP at a Glance, 504 plan, or DEP with academic and behavior goals for reference Behavior, observation, and incident logs from the past 9 weeks/semester Assistive technology (when applicable) Emotion vocabulary cards that provide student-friendly visuals and proper emotion naming (i.e., happy, sad, angry, frustrated, etc.)

(Continued)

One-Minute Meeting Implementation Guide		
Question 3: What challenges or concerns are you experiencing in your class(es) or in our school?		
Duration: 20–22 seconds		
Magnet	Students enrolled at magnet schools experience school through the lens of special or focused interests. Given the academic expectations, school culture, or student's own individual unique proclivities, challenges or concerns may manifest differently depending on the nature of the student. School leaders and instructional teams are tasked with leading magnet school learning environments with specialized programs developed to support students holistically. Depending on the nature of challenges or concerns shared by the students, these leadership teams must mobilize to walk hand in hand with students to make necessary adjustments that render critical change.	With regard to the type of magnet or specialized programs at the school (i.e., STEM, fine and performing arts, CTE, world language, etc.), students can oftentimes experience challenges directly related to their success or lack of in these particular areas. Student-led forums, peer mentoring groups, and peer counselors allow students with natural inclinations toward navigating these challenges to augment the student-centered culture and allow opportunities for authentic dialogue.

*Should students share during Question #3 any information that threatens their or someone else's physical, emotional, social, or academic well-being or jeopardizes their safety or the safety of others, please refer them immediately to licensed professionals who are available to help and support. School leaders should ensure that mental health support services (i.e., school psychologists, external service/community support, school guidance counselors, or peer mediation support teams (if applicable)) are available to assist students and their families as students navigate the perils and challenges of adolescence in the 21st century.

Hearing Ears and Walking Feet

School leaders have a responsibility to their students, teacher leaders, and instructional stakeholders to keep a pulse on what is happening in the school. There are so many tasks required of school leaders from school improvement, school culture development, professional development, personnel supervision, facilities and maintenance, and budget allocation that finding time to interact with each student may seem impossible. Tack onto that list the need to complete classroom walk-throughs and teacher observations, provide sound instructional feedback to lesson plans and instructional strategies, and lead teaching teams/departments in PLCs. The fact of the matter is that these one-on-one, 60-second interactions are the pulse of the school, and carving out 1 minute for each student in the building reaps dividends for each of the aforementioned responsibilities. The key is hearing ears and walking feet before, during, and after the One-Minute Meeting.

The concept of hearing ears is that all data in a school is good data if that data is used to invoke positive change. School leaders observe, engage, and mitigate hundreds of interactions a day; however, when one takes a moment to hear the essence of those interactions, it moves the experience from mere observation to an opportunity for improvement. Of course, these interactions cannot be viewed or dealt with from the principal's office. Walking feet are one of the most powerful school improvement tools for a school leader because they take a leader to all the places where these interactions are occurring. From the cafeteria to the media center and the ball field to the local community center, school leaders must go where the students are to see the full effect of the One-Minute Meeting conversations. Hogan (2018) expressed, "Each and every interaction that is made on the way to and from school and at school in a classroom, hallway, office, lunchroom, playground, or gym can contribute to a student's needs being met. The importance of building relationships goes back to the age-old saying, Kids don't care how much you know until they know how much you care." Before, during, and after the One-Minute Meeting, school leaders should take advantage of monitoring the cafeteria, greeting students at buses in the morning, and engaging with students during after-school or extracurricular events using one of the following phrases:

Hearing Ears and Walking Feet Phrases for the One-Minute Meeting	
Before the One-Minute Meeting	• Hey (insert student's name!) I cannot wait to meet with you during our One-Minute Meeting so I can hear more about (insert student accomplishment).
	• Think about (insert behavior) and let's discuss this during our upcoming One-Minute Meeting.
	• I love that idea (insert student's name)! Be sure to bring that up during our One-Minute Meeting.
During the One-Minute Meeting	• Thank you so much for sharing that with me (insert student's name).
	• The last time we met, you shared (insert information). Can you tell me a little more about how that is going?
	• I will be checking in on you from time to time to make sure you are staying on track with (insert specific goal).
	• If you see me in the hallway, gym, at lockers, etc., do not hesitate to let me know if you are still experiencing a problem with (insert specific challenge/concern).
After the One-Minute Meeting	• Hey (insert student's name)! How is (insert specific goal) going?
	• Remember when we met, you said (insert information)? Is your behavior now lining up with that?
	• You shared with me that you were so proud of (insert information). I want you to keep it up so that we have more to celebrate during our next One-Minute Meeting.

The One-Minute Meeting is more than a program; rather, it is a process. The level of commitment to the process reveals the type of growth a school can experience when student leaders, teacher leaders, and school leaders commit to embracing the students' voices and experiences as the cornerstone for insight, improvement, and impact within a school.

One-Minute Challenge:
Understanding emotional capacity and having the right strategies to cope with those emotions is a struggle for many students in schools today. As an ILT, choose three classrooms in your school. These can be three classrooms that are experiencing management difficulties, three classrooms that are implementing a new instructional strategy or program, or three diverse classrooms representing different age groups. Take 1 minute and walk-through each class. During the walk-through, jot down each emotion that is observed overtly or inadvertently from student-to-student interactions only. Following the three walk-throughs, convene with the team and compile a list of all of the emotions displayed by students. As a team, determine if there are sufficient and effective protocols for students to deal with these emotions, sound professional development to increase teacher effectiveness in light of these emotions, and ample resources for students to work through these emotions.

One-Minute Post-Pandemic Strategy
The impact of this global pandemic is a historical occurrence that caused many to hyper-visualize inequities in the educational system. As challenges and concerns are highlighted by students through the One-Minute Meeting process, remind yourself and members of the team that your students' emotional capacity may be shallow due to the impact of the pandemic. Discussing and planning for these potential challenges as a team will help your school's stakeholders better prepare to meet students' needs.

PART 4 THE STRATEGY

10

Mobilizing the Instructional Leadership Team

One-Minute Reflection Question:
Why is the well-planned and immersive preparation of the stakeholders on the ILT critical in implementing the One-Minute Meeting process in a school?

In this chapter, the school leader will begin developing a strategic plan for implementing the One-Minute Meeting process successfully in the school setting. With specific attention given to the ILT and its role in preserving the integrity of the process, the One-Minute Meeting can be implemented seamlessly given the number of students and time lines allotted. The ILT sets the stage for a majority of the pedagogical, curriculum, and academic initiatives within any school building. Ensuring that the individuals on this team are properly trained and authentically engaged in executing the One-Minute Meeting magnifies its effect on the school as a whole. The school leader is the lead facilitator and lead learner in the journey toward developing and honing the One-Minute Meeting to meet the specific needs of students and schools. Teamwork, intentionality, and high levels of accountability among the members of the ILT allow each minute spent with a student to produce resounding results.

How can we do any more?
—A good-hearted but burned-out third-grade teacher

It was one of those days at FT Elementary that as a principal you immediately recognize as being one of "those days." There was a late bus, which caused the attendance to be submitted past the deadline to the district office. Two parents had gotten into a not-so-favorable verbal exchange in the car rider line, which caused our school resource officer to write them both civil citations. One of my favorite first graders, whose parents were going through a divorce, had locked himself in the boys' bathroom, and our only resident custodian/counselor who happened to be male had called in sick. This left his teacher, teacher assistant, our assistant principal, and me (all female) to try and coax him out from the entrance. Yes, it was one of those days, and I needed approximately four of me to be able to tackle everything efficiently. The evening prior to this impending storm, I had sent our ILT a reminder email letting the group know that we would be meeting immediately after school to discuss our game plan for implementing the One-Minute Meeting. My goal was for each of our team members to be fully engaged and knowledgeable about all aspects of the One-Minute Meeting. To ensure that we had total fidelity in implementing the process, the team members would have the opportunity to see the One-Minute Meeting in action, and I was convinced that they would see the value in this process. Not only would they jump at the opportunity to connect with our students on a one-on-one level, but they would also be the school champions for rebuilding and restructuring the transformative student relationships at FT Elementary! I would soon see that this was not the case at all.

I arrived at the team meeting out of breath and mentally exhausted from the day's events. I had to admit that seeing the last late bus that afternoon afforded me a well-deserved, 5-second sigh of relief that our students were getting home safely and that our teachers would have time to refuel and reenergize before another school day tomorrow. Walking through the doors of our media center, however, I could immediately sense that I was the only one reveling in fleeting relief. I walked straight into a conversation between our teacher of the year and our instructional facilitator debating whether it was the full moon, the fast-approaching spring break, or simply that everyone in the building was tired that had caused such a chaotic day. As I passed out the folders I had meticulously put together, I caught quick glimpses of the eye rolls and exchanges skirting across the tables. Choosing not to acknowledge any of that, I asserted, "Thank you all for joining us this afternoon. We have been on this transformation journey for several months now, and soon we are going to start a process at FT Elementary that is truly going to help us better understand and respond to our students. I know that you all have seen me conducting the One-Minute Meetings in the hallways. I have shared data with you gleaned from those meetings, and many of you have even shared with me what some of our students are saying about the One-Minute Meetings. Now, it is time for you all to become active participants in this process. As leaders across our school, it is critical that you begin to experience our students as critical stakeholders, and the One-Minute Meeting offers just such an opportunity. Today, I am going to train you on what the One-Minute Meeting looks like and how it is conducted and help you prepare to conduct One-Minute Meetings with one grade level. Who's ready?!" I opened my arms excitedly, anticipating the shouts and squeals of avid confirmation. Instead, crickets.

I opened my arms wider with emphasis, hoping that it would simply take my extraordinary ILT a moment to grasp this momentous occasion. Then I closed my arms and listened as our lead third-grade teacher said, "Dr. Hemphill, this sounds like a great idea. We know the One-Minute Meeting works, and we are grateful that you take the time as our leader to meet with each student in the building. But we are swamped, Dr. Hemphill. Between reading diagnostics, writing assessments, PLC exemplars, and spring parent-teacher conferences coming up, it is a lot. I think I speak for all the teachers at least when I ask, *How can we do any more?*"

I took another deep but professional sigh before responding. "I don't know how, but we will find a way because our students have already shown us that they have a lot to say about teaching and learning around here and now we must find a way to listen."

And that is exactly what we did. The ILT worked that afternoon to develop a compromise that involved select teachers shadowing our assistant principal, instructional facilitator, and me during one round of One-Minute Meetings before taking on a class on their own. Once they completed a round of meetings with one class, they would share their experiences with another colleague and train that teacher to conduct the meetings. The One-Minute Meeting "train the trainer" process worked well because it not only freed up time in the short term but also empowered our teacher leaders for the long term. Sometimes, it is not about asking how you can do more but how you can do less with more impact.

Connecting the Mission Statement

As mentioned in Chapter 3, the mission statement should serve as more than mere words on the cover sheet of the school improvement plan; it should provide a school community with a solid framework upon which all stakeholders are able to navigate the daily work that happens in the building, who the work is impacting, and what value the work brings to all involved. Once a mission statement is adopted by a school community, the school leader must model the mission, work to develop accountability measures for the mission, and provide consistent opportunities to grow leaders in and around the mission statement. The ILT represents direct extensions of school leadership and should work in close proximity with the meaning of the mission in their daily work. As transformational school leaders seeking to implement the One-Minute Meeting into a school, ILT members should be deeply involved in understanding a school's history over time to fully understand the effect that the One-Minute Meeting can have on students, teaching, and learning.

Every school has a history, even newly constructed or newly developed schools. Within that history are its embedded traditions, practiced and perceived cultures, and, oftentimes, laundry lists of personnel who have come and gone over the years. When introducing the One-Minute Meeting to an ILT, the history is the quintessential place to start in that it frames the mission statement to the process itself. According to Ravitch (2000),

> History helps us understand educational issues. We cannot understand where we are heading without knowing where we have been. We live now with decisions and policies that were made long ago. Before we attempt to reform present practices, we must try to learn why those decisions were made and to understand the consequences of past policies. History does not tell us the answers to our questions, but it helps to inform us so that we might make better decisions in the future.

Connecting the mission statement to the One-Minute Meeting means understanding where a school and the people connected to it have been. What has the surrounding community dealt with over the years that affected the school? How have the children in the building been perceived throughout the district or community over the years? How has the narrative of the school's test scores and data been told and to whom? Ravitch (2000) was correct when she stated that knowing a school's history does not inform the school leaders or the ILT of the answers to any of those questions, but it certainly assists the team in ensuring that the One-Minute Meeting is positioned to improve teaching and learning conditions for children. Mission-driven leaders understand that there are distinct behaviors associated with the answers to the aforementioned questions—behaviors exhibited on a consistent basis by stakeholders at every level.

When a leader is able to shift the behaviors in the direction that promotes, uplifts, and supports the mission statement, authentic transformation begins to take place. Kustigian (2013) alluded to this phenomenon when he stated, "Mission driven leaders shape behavior over time by utilizing many forms of leadership techniques and balancing concern for production (production equals student achievement in education) with concern for staff. Mission driven leaders use behavior theory to better understand subordinates and how to best communicate the mission and vision for the organization." Communicating the mission statement is key, particularly when it comes to new initiatives or processes that challenge the traditional way of operating in a school. As humans, school stakeholders tend to gravitate toward what is comfortable and what they have always done in the past to achieve results. Transforming a school is so deeply embedded in understanding and navigating people's patterns. School leaders seeking to create new patterns must first identify behaviors that do not align with the mission statement and work intently with the members of the leadership team to help them truly make those connections toward a new understanding.

Kustigian (2013) went on to assert that "mission driven leaders constantly look for ways to intellectually stimulate members of an organization. Mission driven leaders strive to create conditions in which people are so devoted to the mission that they will do just about anything. Intellectually stimulating employees and providing academic challenges motivate individuals towards common goals." Understanding the leadership team and all those connected with the mission statement helps a school leader ascertain the best strategy for introducing a concept like the One-Minute Meeting, exposing stakeholders to the benefits for students once implemented, and igniting a passion inside them to intrinsically want to embrace the process. School leaders who invest time in building professional relationships with the members of their leadership teams glean valuable insight into what motivates team members, what fears they possess regarding implementing the process, and what pitfalls they have experienced in the past, so as not to experience them again. Once the instructional leadership team members are positioned to embrace the mission statement with fresh insight and open mindsets, then initiatives such as the One-Minute Meeting can be easily introduced and embraced.

Practice Makes Pragmatic

Building culture is perhaps one of the greatest challenges set before school leaders who are tasked with transforming schools and connecting the mission statement to daily operations and expectations; it is a powerful step in the right direction. As school leaders mobilize their instructional leadership teams and SITs to lead the mission, it is critical that team members understand that a student-centered culture that practices the One-Minute Meeting leads to interactions that consistently communicate that students matter in every way. Fenton (2019), in his article titled "New Leaders for New Schools: Forming Aligned Instructional Leadership Teams," purported, "In their interactions with other teachers, leadership team members must constantly reinforce the messages that all children are capable of academic success and that it is the responsibility of adults to help them achieve." ILTs model the way with every handshake, every high five, every classroom walk-through, every PLC meeting, and every assembly or pep rally. Through these interactions, school leaders must be overt and intentional in communicating how and why messages of student success matter. From the way that students are greeted at the door in the morning, to the way in which constructive feedback on their learning is given, in order to make huge strides toward a student-centered culture, there must be a commitment to even the most minute of details among adults.

Time is one of the greatest assets for school leaders seeking to implement the One-Minute Meeting process in their buildings. Habits, especially effective ones, are formed over the course of time through a commitment to practicing the new skill or mindset until it eventually becomes a habit. School leaders who maximize time understand that the more stakeholders in the building understand the mission, the greater the level of accountability. For instance, imagine a school's lead instructional team or SIT working diligently with school stakeholders to develop a mission statement devoted to positive peer-to-peer interactions. The desired type of interactions between and among students is clearly delineated within the mission statement, including ways in which students will be taught how to interact and how they will be held accountable when and if they do not comply. At the beginning of the school year, four teacher leaders were assigned to afternoon bus duty, and they are responsible for ensuring that students exit the building in an orderly fashion, board the buses safely, and dismiss in a timely manner. During afternoon dismissal one afternoon, two of the teachers noticed a group of middle school students congregating right in front of the bus door. Upon approaching the group of now boisterous seventh and eighth graders, the teacher leaders noticed that two students in particular were exchanging demeaning and derogatory words with one another. Based on their prior training on the mission statement and their commitment to upholding the tenets within, both teachers sprang into action by quickly dismissing the onlookers to their appropriate buses, separating the two students, and addressing the objectionable behavior with plans to follow up that evening and in the morning for conflict mediation. This is one example of how practicing the mission statement leads to pragmatic processes throughout the building to ensure that the mission statement is realized among all stakeholders.

Commitment to the mission statement also includes the efficient use of data to inform behavior. Fenton (2019) upheld this tenet by stating, "Highly effective principals also seek to create a broad understanding across their faculty that service on the leadership team is both a reward for demonstrated effectiveness (identified by observations and student learning data) and an opportunity for professional learning." For the One-Minute Meeting to have the greatest impact, school leaders should position members of the ILT or the SIT to learn through the process of implementation. This includes providing opportunities for stakeholders to observe the process of meeting with individual students, allowing them to assist in preparing the One-Minute Meeting mobile cart, and providing them with schedules prior to beginning the One-Minute Meeting to aid in their understanding of preparation. By walking alongside lead team members through the process of implementation, school leaders create natural professional learning opportunities that highlight the high level of investment that a school can have in learning from its students. The effectiveness of the One-Minute Meeting process is directly related to high levels of intentional practice, consistent accountability, and commitment to authentic learning for students and adults alike. With the school leader empowering and nurturing a culture of true student-centered transformation, the One-Minute Meeting can help to grow learning communities that are stitched together with compassion for the teaching and learning experience versus mere compliance to do school the way it has always been done.

Scheduling the School Leader

The academic research pendulum is swinging in the direction of distributive leadership to have a greater impact within schools and learning communities. More and more schools of thought are abandoning the top-down leadership structure and replacing it with strategies and resources that grow individuals where they are. In an effort to add to stakeholders' tool kits, school leaders ultimately strengthen the team as a whole by having the time to differentiate conversations, resources, and support for individuals. The universal lynchpin, however, to these transformational theories are leaders who carry within themselves the capacity, insight, and overall flexibility to provide a landscape upon which these theories can be practiced without fear of failure. To nurture a culture that is in need of an evolution, a school leader must be fully present and available to provide support and feedback and simply maximize learning moments for all stakeholders involved in the One-Minute Meeting. Purposeful scheduling is essential for the school leader to keep at the forefront of the implementation of this process, particularly when introducing the One-Minute Meeting into the school setting. In much the same manner that a school leader will schedule principals meetings at the district level, parent-teacher conferences, and post-observation conversations with teacher leaders, scheduling the One-Minute Meeting demands a level of intentionality to experience success.

By scheduling a specific time to prepare and implement this process, school leaders have the freedom to fully assign their mental energy to the development of the team and the feedback gleaned from students. With so many issues, activities, and distractions that arise during a school day, a school leader's undivided attention is the most precious commodity that can be devoted to this transformation process. Austin et al. (2018) alluded to the delicate balance of leadership roles and responsibilities by stating,

> Form an instructional leadership team of teacher leaders to identify teaching and learning challenges in your building. This same team can be used to support teachers in solving these challenges. Such a team can help build its own instructional leadership skills while expanding your capacity to provide the kind of support that your teachers and students need and deserve.

When students and teachers know that their leader is fully present, the commitment to the process is heightened, and they will be much more apt to share their celebrations, as well as their challenges. Without these opportunities, school leaders will find it much more difficult to leverage their leadership or SITs on certain student challenges, and it will be nearly impossible to gain the trust of the students when implementing the One-Minute Meeting. Time literally holds the key to the success of any massive shift in organizational culture, and it holds true when it comes to school leader scheduling and protecting the time necessary to spend with students and teachers involved in the One-Minute Meeting process.

Scheduling as a school leader is an art form amid the plethora of high-priority issues that demand the leader's attention. Mastering this skill requires that norms be established upfront, communicated clearly, and held to the highest level of accountability. To assist school leaders in the process, the following are suggestions for establishing a landscape that makes it easier for school leaders to schedule with intentionality:

Scheduling Tips for the School Leader

1. Set aside time with the assistant principal(s) and others responsible for discipline and evaluation in the building. Explain to them that you will be beginning the One-Minute Meeting process and that you will need them to cover office and classroom calls, impromptu parent meetings, and other low-level emergencies during that time. Frame this as an opportunity for aspiring principals to take the helm and inform them that you will be available to meet prior to your One-Minute Meetings to discuss any questions or concerns they might have to ensure their success. Offer to meet with them after the culmination of the One-Minute Meetings to discuss their experiences and listen to their reflections to grow their leadership capacity.

2. Meet with your front office manager and/or data manager to discuss the implementation of the One-Minute Meeting. Explain that you will be "offline" during your meetings with students and that the assistant principal(s) or other disciplinary stakeholders will be available during that time. Provide these individuals with a list of stakeholders who should be directed to you immediately if they initiate contact while you are in a One-Minute Meeting (i.e., the district superintendent, the president of the United States). Also, provide your front line with potential responses to angry parents who demand to see the principal. Examples include the following: "Our principal has devoted today to meet with our students and hear their concerns and celebrations about our school. She/e will be available later today or tomorrow if you would like to schedule something."

3. During a faculty meeting or professional development training, take time to talk with the faculty and staff about the implementation of the One-Minute Meeting. Not only will the teachers glean valuable feedback about the students' experience in their classrooms, but it will also help to improve teaching and learning conditions as a school. Training the students to embrace and be aware of the process

will require help from teacher leaders, particularly when meetings are being conducted in the hallway. Talk with teachers about helping students navigate through the halls quietly when they see One-Minute Meetings occurring. Also, because students will be sharing their biggest celebrations and their greatest challenges, talk with students about the importance of confidentiality and allow them to brainstorm ways that they can protect it for all students. These discussions will lay the groundwork for students to support the One-Minute Meeting as a student body; they will also help them understand the magnitude of their time in the chair.

Providing clear expectations and supports for the One-Minute Meeting allows school leaders to lead from within and take their school's stakeholders along with them on the path to transformation. Once the proper time protections have been established for this process, the work of preparation and implementation can begin seamlessly. The One-Minute Meeting may be 60 seconds in structure, but that 60 seconds reaps an infinite amount of reward for growth as a learning community!

One-Minute Challenge:
To determine how to approach intentional scheduling, take an inventory of the ways in which you are currently spending your time. Retrieve your calendar from a typical workweek. First, take 1 minute to ascertain what you are spending the greatest amount of time on as a school leader. Where are you devoting your time in the building? What external processes are holding your time hostage? How much time overall is being spent in classrooms and developing the processes of teaching and learning? Then take 1 minute to locate opportunities in your schedule to set aside protected time to meet with students for the One-Minute Meeting. Highlight those places on the calendar and then make a short bulleted list of what stakeholders you need to meet with to fully protect that time. This is the beginning of your strategic plan for implementation. Establishing a strategic vision for the transformative process allows you to clear a path toward achieving your goals, and tackling your schedule is the first critical step!

One-Minute Post-Pandemic Strategy

After years of research, discussion, and debate around the definition and implementation of innovation, schools across the country were prompted by COVID-19 to move expeditiously in putting innovative practice to work. In redesigning teaching and learning in a post-pandemic society, school leaders must think earnestly and innovatively about the time teacher leaders are given to plan for a new normal. Work intentionally with your ILT and school improvement teams to rethink the approach to scheduling, professional learning teams (PLTs), and master scheduling to ensure that teacher leaders have adequate support to plan, redesign, and prepare for reaching all students.

Communicating With Teacher Leaders

One-Minute Reflection Question:
What role does effective communication with teacher leaders play in implementing the One-Minute Meeting process effectively?

In this chapter, the school leader will reflect deeply on the critical role that teacher leaders serve in the implementation of schoolwide, transformative initiatives. Understanding how to communicate with teacher leaders to establish baseline expectations for processes like the One-Minute Meeting develops consistency in implementation, thus making the experience more impactful for students. School leaders who then use that understanding to extend those expectations ultimately create opportunities for autonomy, feedback, and reflection from and among teacher leaders in their learning communities. This further hones the process and engages all stakeholders in a cycle of continuous improvement, which truly differentiates the One-Minute Meeting process in meeting the specific needs of a leader's students and school. Communication with teacher leaders is a powerful factor in the One-Minute Meeting process that can either enhance or destroy its overall effectiveness. School leaders who are intent in their leadership to communicate meaningfully and authentically with teacher leaders as it relates to the One-Minute Meeting process will experience incredible improvement in their learning communities.

> *It just makes sense for children.*
> **—A now enlightened fifth-grade teacher**

I t was 1 month before the EOG tests, and I had to admit that I was a little nervous. It was our first year as a codified school family, and while we had moved the needle significantly in terms of processes, procedures, teaching, learning, and culture, we still had to match wits with the upper grades' standardized tests at the end of the school year. There was no expense in mental or academic energy spared to ensure that our students, teachers, and parents were fully immersed in creating conditions of success for our students. Two weeks prior, we had hosted a very successful EOG boot camp for our school family. We invited all of our third-, fourth-, and fifth-grade students and their families to our school one evening to participate in an academic training camp that allowed them to practice and prepare for the big day. We transformed our cafeteria into a mess hall; the fourth- and fifth-grade hallway became an obstacle course that could only be defeated by answering multiple-choice math and ELA questions; the nurse's station was a pit stop where parents were informed about the true importance of a healthy dinner the night before the test, as well as a good night's sleep; our gym was the culminating activity with family and friends participating in games, exercises, and activities that could be done to stimulate our students' brains during the week of testing that did not involve spending countless hours staring at digital devices or zoning in on the television. We were determined to arm our students and their parents/ guardians with as much information as possible to empower them during this critical time in the school year!

Our team members had just finished their last round of One-Minute Meetings the day before, and our assistant principal and I were reflecting on the data and feedback from our students in my office. Ms. Greenwich entered from the side door that joined our offices with a surprised and yet perplexed look on her face as she dumped her mountain of notebooks, papers, laptop, and pack of Nabs on her desk. I immediately noticed her face when I looked up from the fifth-grade math data I had been pouring over and said, "Are you okay?" Ms. Greenwich plopped down in the armed chair and replied, "You will never guess what I just witnessed."

While this is a statement in school leadership that instantly conjures a plethora of potential positive and negative possibilities, I refrained from leaping straight to the negative, and with as much hope and excitement as I could muster, I said, "Tell me everything!"

Ms. Greenwich stated that she had been doing her final round of teacher observations that afternoon to complete her summative evaluations, and when she entered Ms. Lesley's room, she was immediately taken aback by what she'd observed. Ms. Lesley was a stellar mathematics teacher, but she was extremely set in her ways. Her response to ongoing district professional development was often negative, and she openly shared her retorts with the facilitator, her colleagues, or anyone who would listen about why we needed professional development when the old strategies worked just fine with students. Ms. Lesley had been vocal about the One-Minute Meeting implementation earlier that school year, openly stating during a staff meeting that "children did not know what was good for them" and that "it was a waste of time to even consider the opinions of children who did not care about their education anyway."

Ms. Greenwich went on to say that as she entered the classroom, the students were sitting in pairs around the room with whiteboards and Expo markers. There were sample EOG questions taped to the walls, the chairs, the windows, and even on Ms. Lesley's desk, and students were rotating around the room, tackling the problems, finding common solutions, and discussing with the partners why they chose the mathematical formula or strategy to solve a particular problem. They then had to decide, given four options on a multiple-choice test, how they would narrow the options based on the strategy they chose and conclusively check their work. It was an authentic student-centered discussion on mathematical content and not one student even noticed that Ms. Greenwich had entered the room to observe. But what caught Ms. Greenwich's attention next was nothing short of an educational miracle. When she glanced toward the back of the room at Ms. Lesley's kidney table, she noticed Ms. Lesley and a student huddled over a piece of paper. Both the student and the teacher were enthralled in conversation, with Ms. Lesley asking a question and the student scribbling out things on the paper and then erasing and scribbling again.

This went on for about 1 minute, and when the student finally looked up and said, "Oh! That's why I missed that problem!"

Ms. Greenwich heard the teacher say, "No worries! Now you know what you can do better next time, and I want you to remember that strategy and practice it for the EOGs coming up." Ms. Lesley handed the student the paper, looked on her class roster, called a name, and the next student went bouncing toward the back of the room with paper in hand.

After 60 seconds, Ms. Lesley would send the student off with a positive affirmation and call another name to her kidney table. This process went on for 5 minutes."

At the end of the observation, Ms. Greenwich said she went over to let Ms. Lesley know that it was a wonderful observation and inquired as to what she was doing with each student and the papers they were discussing.

Ms. Lesley laughed and said, "Well I decided to do One-Minute Meetings with my students in math. Based on the scores of the last exam, a majority of the students are still struggling with fractions, but they each had different problem sets they were struggling with. The One-Minute Meeting allows me to address specific problems and strategies quickly so I can show them what they missed, allow them to fix their thinking around those problem sets, and do a quick practice. It's been working, and the students love it! It just makes sense for children." Ms. Greenwich said she thanked Ms. Lesley for all her hard work and left the classroom quickly, making a beeline straight to the main office for our meeting. As she finished the story, Ms. Greenwich noticed that my jaw was now sitting atop my desk. Perhaps the One-Minute Meeting was more than simply a conduit to glean student feedback. Perhaps it was a catalyst for real change for students *and* teachers as well!

True School Improvement From the Inside Out

School improvement is one of the most rewarding, yet arduous, undertakings when it comes to shifting the mindsets and ideals of not only the stakeholders inside the building but also extending that message to external stakeholders. But true school improvement starts on the inside of any learning community. It is the students—their experiences, the stories they share with the parents or guardians as soon as they get in the car in the afternoon, or the answers to "how was your day today?"—that begin to modify parents' notions and understandings of how their children's schools are truly changing. Students have an up close and personal experience with the learning community on a daily basis, and as the recipients of carefully planned lessons, the participants in problem-based learning activities, experiments, and after-school activities, they are able to help write the narrative for school change in the direction of their experiences. For teacher leaders, it is no different. It is how they experience the school day and the messages that have been communicated to them by their school leader and leadership team; it is the information and leverage they have been given to create classrooms that engage and inspire that genuinely influence their narratives. Strategic communication has the power to shift those narratives in the direction of success if school leaders carefully consider how to bring teacher leaders along on the journey versus force-feeding them ill-thought-out and poorly constructed messages that do not consider their needs as professionals.

In preparation for introducing learning communities to the One-Minute Meeting process, school leaders, SITs, and/or leadership teams must invest time up front to develop a communication plan that specifically addresses teacher leaders' needs. Implementation of the One-Minute Meeting is a bold but necessary leadership move. Because humans often do not adapt well to change, it is important to remember that "sometimes, education leaders must choose between doing what's popular or doing what's needed to create a more equitable, effective education system for the future. It's a balancing act" (Johnson, 2015). In most cases, the One-Minute Meeting will be a new concept for not only the learning community but also the stakeholders who will be charged with sustaining it, so it is paramount that teacher leaders are able to clearly and easily see the benefits for not only students but also their classrooms. According to Johnson (2015), school leaders must keep in mind that "sometimes, strong, well-thought-out messaging can be useful—in conveying specific kinds of new information, for example, or in countering misperceptions or gaps in knowledge among the broader public."

When communicating the potential significance of the One-Minute Meeting for your school, establish a common language that is familiar to teacher leaders across grade levels and departments. Consider school counselors, data managers, cafeteria workers, and custodians in your messaging so that all stakeholders are able to approach the One-Minute Meeting with a baseline understanding of what it is and how students will be involved. As the leadership team engages in the process for the first time, take the necessary time to archive student experiences and interactions that demonstrate a sincere change in practice, particularly in teaching and learning. Find innovative ways to share those interactions with teacher leaders either via email, through video journaling, or in public forums (i.e., staff meetings, PLCs, etc.). The more opportunities that the school leader has to put the One-Minute Meeting in front of teacher leaders initially, the more feedback can be gleaned to alter processes and expectations before moving into schoolwide implementation. The One-Minute Meeting is a living, breathing framework that can be revised to meet the needs of the students and the school, and who better to offer firsthand evaluation than those professionals spending the most face time with our student stakeholders?

Perhaps one of the most imperative strategies for school leaders, as it relates to communicating with teacher leaders, is taking advantage of opportunities to embrace the realism of the teacher leader experience. School leaders are tasked with facing an overabundance of constant problems, questions, and obstacles on a daily basis; however, it is how one finesses the response to each of these issues that can make or break a school's culture overall. Addressing the truth about a specific learning community—the good, the bad, and the ugly—can literally put a school leader in a better position to develop more effective communication that positively ignites teacher leaders! Johnson (2015) eloquently conveyed this point by asserting,

> Let people in on how hard this is. The mission facing education today is daunting: We have to do a much better job educating all our children to live and thrive in a world that is changing in ways we often struggle to understand. People need to understand that improving schools doesn't happen with a wave of a wand; change always comes with risks, costs, and trade-offs.

Teacher leaders respect the truth. They respect a school leader who addresses the truth but also offers tangible, realistic, and urgent solutions to those truths to create safe, engaging, and future-focused spaces for students to learn and teachers to teach. When communicating with teacher leaders about the implementation of the One-Minute Meeting process, hit the realities head-on. Discuss the potential shortage of human capital to reach all the students, mention the lack of buy-in that will occur from students at first, and embrace the fact that there is simply not enough time in the school day to do all the things that are mandated or asked of teacher leaders. Then, once those pink elephants have been called out by name, invite them to dance with each and every stakeholder as one works to develop solutions, strategies, and procedures that will allow the One-Minute Meeting process to thrive in the learning community as a solution toward not only hearing but also truly listening to our students and their experiences.

More Than a Memo

Communicating with teacher leaders regarding the One-Minute Meeting, particularly when introducing the concept, is a significant step in the transformation process for any learning community. School leaders must keep in mind that the process itself is foreign for most educators and that it will take time for stakeholders to fully understand, embrace, and execute the One-Minute Meeting at its most optimal level. Schoolwide implementation requires a carefully designed and well-thought-out plan of action to ensure that all leadership team members are working in tandem to communicate consistent expectations of teacher leaders and their students, as well as information that is readily available and accurate. The following is a sample communication plan for implementing the One-Minute Meeting that is helpful for considering all potential factors of the process itself.

Communication Plan for Implementing the One-Minute Meeting

Type	Target Stakeholders	Frequency	Purpose	Persons Responsible
Faculty/Staff Meetings	Teacher leaders	Monthly	To introduce the high-level effect of the One-Minute Meeting, as well as communicate the specific needs of the school based on data, surveys, and school or district initiatives	School leader, lead instructional team, or SIT
PLCs or Department Meetings	Teacher leaders	Monthly	To specifically discuss how the One-Minute Meeting will affect the schedule, address a specific student or grade level/department needs, and provide opportunities for teacher leader feedback, questions, and concerns	Lead instructional team and lead teacher leaders for each grade level or department
Email/Memo	Teacher leaders	Week before One-Minute Meetings begin and during as necessary (i.e., schedule conflicts)	To provide high-level reminders of when the One-Minute Meeting will begin, schedule for meeting with each grade level or department, and high-level reminders for teacher leaders, support staff, and front office staff	School leader and administrative team
Morning/ Afternoon Announcements	Student leaders	On the day One-Minute Meetings begin and throughout the process	To introduce students to the concept of the One-Minute Meeting, set expectations for each student to participate, and set high-level expectations for movement throughout the building as One-Minute Meetings are being conducted	School leader and administrative team

(Continued)

Communication Plan for Implementing the One-Minute Meeting (*Continued*)

Type	Target Stakeholders	Frequency	Purpose	Persons Responsible
Morning/ Afternoon Duty/ Hallway Monitoring	Student leaders	Ongoing	To serve as follow-ups with individual students after the One-Minute Meetings have been conducted and to offer encouragement, support, and feedback based on individual student needs	School leader, lead instructional team, or SIT
Parent Newsletter	Parents/ Guardians/ Community	Week before One-Minute Meetings begin	To introduce the high-level effect of the One-Minute Meeting, set anticipatory expectations for students prior to the One-Minute Meeting rounds, as well as remind parents that their children's voices matter in the learning community	School leader and lead instructional team

Sample One-Minute Meeting Memo

Greetings teacher leaders!

Happy Monday, and I hope that you and your students are ready for a phenomenal week of teaching and learning. This week we will begin our first round of One-Minute Meetings! Thank you again for your participation in our preliminary discussions during last month's faculty meeting. I know that our school will benefit from the One-Minute Meeting process and our taking the time to listen to our most valued stakeholders: our students. As a reminder, there is no need for you to prepare ancillary lessons or change your class schedule. I will have the mobile office set up on your hallway first thing in the morning, and I will begin by entering your classroom and tapping the first student on your class roster on the shoulder. We will exit quietly so as not to disturb your instruction. Once we wrap up the first student, s/he will go in and tap the next student, so on and so forth until we reach the end of the list.

Our administrative team will be making an important announcement regarding the One-Minute Meeting during morning announcements tomorrow so that students will know what to expect and how these meetings will impact them and our school. If your students have specific questions, please take a few moments to address their inquiries or let me or a member of our ILT know to stop by your classroom. We are happy to assist you and the students in any way!

Below you will find the schedule for One-Minute Meetings for this week:

All One-Minute Meeting rotations will begin immediately after morning announcements at 8:45 a.m.

Tuesday—Third-grade classes

8:45 a.m.—Mrs. Melvin's Class
9:45 a.m.—Mr. Beasley's Class
10:45 a.m.—Mrs. Myer's Class

11:45 a.m.—Break for lunch
12:45 p.m.—Mrs. Austin's Class
1:45 p.m.—Mrs. Davis's Class

Wednesday—Fourth-grade classes

8:45 a.m.—Mr. Triplett's Class
9:45 a.m.—Mrs. Smith's Class
10:45 a.m.—Ms. Robbin's Class

11:45 a.m.—Break for lunch
12:45 p.m.—Mrs. McDougald's Class
1:45 p.m.—Ms. Blackwell's Class

Thursday—Fifth-grade classes

8:45 a.m.—Dr. Ray's Class
9:45 a.m.—Mrs. Kickasola's Class
10:45 a.m.—Mrs. McRae's Class

11:45 a.m.—Break for lunch
12:45 p.m.—Mrs. Harrison's Class
1:45 p.m.—Mr. Ferrell's Class

Thank you in advance for your commitment to and support of innovative practices at FT Elementary. Your knowledge and expertise are invaluable to our journey of transformation, and we cannot wait to share the outcomes of this first round of One-Minute Meetings with each of you. If you have any questions or concerns, do not hesitate to let us know. Have a stellar remainder of the week!

From Automatic to Autonomy

As the school leader develops sound systems of communication to and among teacher leaders, the learning community will begin to experience a dynamic upsurge in its level of awareness of teaching and learning. School leaders who are intentional in their messaging to teacher leaders will begin to observe that the processes and procedures for instructional planning and building classroom culture will shift as well. Communication is powerful because each individual has the unique opportunity to interpret the message and draw out specific meaning that relates to their experiences. For instance, upon first hearing that their school is going to implement the One-Minute Meeting process, one teacher leader may interpret that as a unique opportunity to learn more about her/his students while another teacher leader may interpret the process as more work added to already overloaded responsibilities. With the implementation of any new initiative, there will be eager followers and those who are resistant; however, it is those eager teacher leaders who will experience the shift in their teaching and learning more quickly because they see the overall benefit in truly listening to and acting on the feedback from student stakeholders.

For decades, public education has been characterized by a list of rote routines, processes, and procedures carried out by various stakeholders, but particularly teacher leaders. From the manner in which lesson plans are created, to establishing classroom management, or to even administering assessments, these occurrences in schools across the country come automatically to teacher leaders in the field. Day in and day out, teacher leaders perform these tasks automatically and oftentimes without question because that is simply the way that "school" has always been done. Carefully designed and thoughtful communication shifts thinking and shatters automatic behaviors to authentically autonomous ones. When school leaders are able to communicate to a specific teacher how small changes in their level of feedback, instructional strategy, or pedagogy can help ensure student and teacher success, teacher leaders begin to seek this level of communication as a form of professional development. School leaders and their ILT may begin the school year by executing the One-Minute Meeting process themselves, but with intentional communication in word and in deed, teacher leaders will embrace the One-Minute Meeting as their own and begin to actively seek opportunities to implement it themselves.

It is at this level that learning communities move from automatic to autonomous because teacher leaders take up the charge as their own. School leaders are often one or two to a school; however, the number of teacher leaders multiply depending on the size of the school population and needs. The One-Minute Meeting is a living, breathing process that when embraced has the power to elevate teacher leaders to the level of educational experts and professionals who consistently and consciously seek to perfect their craft. According to Harrison and Killion (2007), "Teacher leaders can also be catalysts for change, visionaries who are never content with the status quo but rather always looking for a better way. Teachers who take on the catalyst role feel secure in their own work and have a strong commitment to continual improvement. They pose questions to generate analysis of student learning" Keeping students at the center of the One-Minute Meeting process is critical, but understanding that communication with teacher leaders is the lynchpin toward effective transformation for a learning community is invaluable.

One-Minute Challenge:

It is critical for school leaders and their leadership teams to have real-time, reliable feedback on how teacher leaders are receiving the messages behind schoolwide communication. Pair up each member of the leadership team and instruct them to choose two different teacher leaders in the building who do not work on the same team, in the same department, or in the same vicinity of the school. Ask the team to schedule a convenient time with that teacher leader (no more than 5 minutes) to ask the teacher the following questions:

1. When it comes to communication at (insert school name here), do you feel as if our leadership team communicates effectively and efficiently?
2. How do you feel about the information you receive as it relates to impacting your students, teaching, and learning?
3. In your opinion, how can communication from our leadership team be improved to help you do your job better?

After gathering all of the responses, meet to compile, analyze, and disaggregate the responses to draw out overarching themes, opportunities for improvement, and brainstorm solutions that will enhance communication to and among teacher leaders in your learning community.

One-Minute Post-Pandemic Strategy

Feedback from teacher leaders is critical in designing post-pandemic communication that evokes community change. As many teacher leaders juggle new professional and personal responsibilities in light of the pandemic, work with the ILT and school improvement team to set up regular check-ins with teacher leaders to glean their perspective on communication in the school community. Their insight is critical to ensuring the success of the One-Minute Meeting process with students.

Preparing the Mobile Office

 One-Minute Reflection Question:
How does a well-developed mobile office support the implementation of the One-Minute Meeting process for students?

In this chapter, the school leader will discover the materials necessary for the One-Minute Meeting mobile office and develop her/his own mobile office plan to further contribute to the One-Minute Meeting's success. The mobile office allows the school leader and the ILT to maximize the 60-second time frame by having all necessary data, schedules, rosters, templates, technology, etc., at their fingertips. Preparing the mobile office is the last step in mastering the strategy behind this flexible framework. To ensure that each student receives the full benefit of their time during the One-Minute Meeting, adequate preparation and mobile office development is critical. This process shatters the tradition and infamous connotation of calling students to the main office and innovatively brings the main office to them!

> *Shh! Dr. Hemphill is doing that thing where she asks us what we think about school!*
> **—A precocious kindergarten student**

It had taken our team months to get everyone on board with the One-Minute Meeting. By this point in the school year, FT Elementary had experienced its share of setbacks, naysayers, scheduling conflicts, and even noncompliant student participants, but it seemed that the One-Minute Meeting was making a significant impact. After analyzing the major trends and themes from the last round of One-Minute Meeting responses, the lead instructional team noticed that students were becoming much more vocal and adept at naming their feelings and providing feedback. Teacher leaders were helping students throughout the semester to develop their voices through intentional socioemotional lessons and most were even encouraging students to share their candid thoughts, feelings, and experiences with our team during the upcoming round of meet-ings. The lead instructional team also noticed that student goal setting was helping tremendously as well. Over 60% of the upper-grade students who had verbalized their goals for the third-quarter benchmarks met or surpassed their intended goals in one or more content areas! The power of purposeful, strategic goal setting with our students was actualized through the One-Minute Meeting process, and we were grateful for the learning and leadership lessons we gained as a school family.

I was standing in my permanent office preparing my mobile office for the last round of One-Minute Meetings that school year. I wheeled the now-famous black cart over to my desk and started mentally listing everything I would need for the kindergarten, first-, and second-grade students: class rosters printed that morning for accuracy; last quarter's reading levels and assessment data for each student; last quarter's One-Minute Meeting notes for each student; anecdotal data from teachers, which included specific students they had asked me to speak to about family situations, behavior, or academic progress; and, finally, attendance data for those students who were chronically absent or late. I arranged all of my data folders in the order in which I planned to visit each classroom and then began restocking my Post-it® Notes, pens, pencils, paper clips, and extra scrap paper in case I needed to write a quick note or reminder. I placed these items on the second shelf so that they would be within arm's reach. Lastly, I walked behind my desk and opened up my secret stash of snacks. Conducting One-Minute Meetings requires a fortitude of mental and physical energy, and I wanted to ensure that my energy levels were optimal for our students. I quickly grabbed two packs of peanut butter Nabs, a bottle of water, and some peppermints, placed them inside the hidden compartment within the cart, and leaned back to inspect the almost finished mobile office.

There was only one additional component to the mobile office that I needed to prepare: the principal's desk chair. It was perhaps the most important factor, and the students absolutely loved sitting in this chair as they regaled our team and me with their greatest celebrations and challenges. Whenever our students saw me precariously wheeling my desk chair and the mobile office down the hallway, they knew that it was time for the One-Minute Meetings to begin. They had even become accustomed to being on their best behavior at noise level zero in the hallway when they saw me leaning in intently to listen to other students' responses to the three questions. One first grader who was passing the mobile office on her way to the restroom dramatically covered her ears so as not to hear my conversation with another student after I had made a special morning announcement about respecting the confidentiality of the One-Minute Meeting conferences.

I headed down the long corridor toward Ms. Patillio's classroom. I had acquired a new talent of pushing the mobile cart and pulling the desk chair at the same time in the general direction I was traveling, albeit simply a maneuver to eliminate multiple trips to the main office. I always loved starting the morning with the kindergarten students because their colorful and candid responses to the One-Minute Meeting questions brightened my spirit and gave me hope for the future of society. This morning was no different, and as each little 5-year-old climbed into the principal's desk chair and responded to the questions verbally and some using the emotion vocabulary cards, there seemed to be an overall joyous tone to the experiences our soon-to-be first grad-ers were having at FT Elementary. I had one more class to go to before wrapping up when Ms. Patillio's classroom door swung wide open. Ms. Patillio softly reminded her kinders that they were to be quiet on their way to the cafeteria for lunch before she and her assistant escorted almost 22 little ones down the corridor through the glass double doors. I could see Xavier, a beloved but frequent flyer in the main office, at the back of the line trying to talk to one of his classmates. As they passed me, Xavier made another attempt to get the little girl's attention, and as they walked closer, the now bothered student whipped around, put her finger to her lips, and said, "Shhh! Dr. Hemphill is doing that thing where she asks us what we think about school!" She confidently turned back around, regained her composure, and continued walking toward the cafeteria in complete silence. It was official. The One-Minute Meeting mattered to our students.

The Basics

The main office for any school is the hub or central station of all business, information, exchanges, and direction pertaining to a specific learning community. School leaders work to develop processes and procedures that enhance stakeholders' experiences from the main office. Unfortunately, the main office is traditionally where most school leaders spend the majority of their time interacting with students, teacher leaders, district leaders, parents/guardians, and community members. One of the goals of the One-Minute Meeting is to shatter this tradition by providing opportunities for school leaders to increase visibility, promote accessibility to student stakeholders, and increase time spent where students thrive: the classrooms, gathering spaces, and hallways of the learning community. School leaders who are highly visible and largely accessible are able to model the way much more efficiently with large-scale transformative processes, such as the One-Minute Meeting, versus those school leaders who lead from the main office.

When considering how to begin developing one's mobile office for the One-Minute Meeting, start with the basic necessities of the main office as a foundation. School leaders should carefully consider items and materials that will help to streamline and maximize their 60 seconds with their students. By considering the following reflection questions, school leaders will be better able to ascertain which basic materials or items to include in their starter mobile offices:

Reflection Questions for Preparing the One-Minute Meeting Mobile Office

- What basic office items do you use on a daily basis to organize papers, documents, notebooks, etc.?

- What basic office materials do you use regularly to maximize document or file transport?

- What basic office items do you consider absolutely necessary to maximizing your overall effectiveness and productivity?

Answering these questions is an effective first step in deciding what materials to include in the mobile office. Take time to create a short list of items and materials so that during your first round of implementation necessary changes and revisions can be made to the list. With each round of the One-Minute Meeting implemented in a learning community, putting together the mobile office should become easier, more sustainable, and replicable to other stakeholders who assist in implementing the process as well. The following is a list of common items and materials that can be used to put together the mobile office; however, this list can be revised and edited based on students' needs, specific school dynamics and demographics, and accessibility and protocol.

The One-Minute Mobile Office Starter Kit	
pens or pencils	highlighters
Post-it® Notes	file folders
notepad	paper clips
stapler	stapler remover
tape	laptop/tablet
correctional tape	graph paper (optional)
three-hole punch (optional)	binder notebooks (optional)

Data Collection Tools and Templates

When it comes to data collection tools and templates, the One-Minute Meeting is designed to meet the specific needs of diverse students and the diverse learning community in which they learn, lead, and thrive. School leaders and their ILTs or SITs will work to develop the mission statement based on school, district, local, state, or even national initiatives, which allows the One-Minute Meeting to focus on multiple data sources and assessments. Depending on the instructional, behavioral, cultural, or even extracurricular initiatives at the school, work as a leadership team to decide the mode of data collection that will work most efficiently for students and the learning community. Elementary, middle, and high school students will have different needs when it comes to the feedback and goal setting necessary to help transform their thinking as critical stakeholders in the school. School leaders and their instructional leadership team may choose to focus on literacy goals and assessments for the first quarter or reporting period and then shift to mathematics goals and assessments for the second quarter. Alignment and consistency are key to the One-Minute Meeting, so ensure that the data collection tool or template matches a critical need or school improvement goal that results in transformative change no matter which one is chosen.

The following are various One-Minute Meeting data collection tools and templates suitable for elementary, middle, and high schools that are easily edited and replicable to meet the specific needs of one's learning community.

Data Collection Template

The One-Minute Meeting

Date	Stakeholder Name	Grade Level

Teacher Name	Quarter (circle one)	Room #
	1 2 3 4	

Student Name or ID	Notes

Data Collection Template

The One-Minute Meeting

Date	Stakeholder Name	Grade Level

Teacher Name	Quarter (circle one)	Room #
	1 2 3 4	

Student Name or ID	How are you today?	What is your greatest celebration, or what are you most proud of from the past 9 weeks (quarter/semester?)	What challenges or concerns are you experiencing in your class(es) or our school?

Data Collection Template

The One-Minute Meeting

Date	Stakeholder Name	Grade Level

Homeroom Teacher Name	Quarter (circle one)	Content Area
	1 2 3 4	

Student Name or ID	Notes

Data Collection Template

The One-Minute Meeting

Date	Stakeholder Name	Grade Level

Homeroom Teacher Name	Quarter/Semester (circle one)	Content Area
	1 2 3 4	

Student Name or ID	Benchmark Data	Notes

Data Collection Template

The One-Minute Meeting

Date	Stakeholder Name	Grade Level

Homeroom Teacher Name	Quarter/Semester (circle one)	Graduation Track
	1 2 3 4	

Student Name or ID	How are you today?	What is your greatest celebration, or what are you most proud of from the past 9 weeks (quarter/ semester?)	What challenges or concerns are you experiencing in your class(es) or our school?

Technology

School leaders are leading in a time when technology is literally disrupting every industry on earth and transforming the way that business, communication, and networking is done on a global scale. Fortunately, the world of education understands that technology is a critical component for reaching 21st-century learners, teachers, and leaders and providing them with the tools necessary to compete on a global platform. Technology is also imperative to the success of the One-Minute Meeting process because it allows the school leader and her/his instructional leadership team to collect, share, edit, and download data among multiple stakeholders at the touch of a button. As it relates to the development of the mobile office and implementing the One-Minute Meeting, technology allows school leaders to capture feedback from students quickly while still respecting the 60-second time frame.

When using technology with the One-Minute Meeting, it is important to be clear on the purpose of its use prior to introducing it to the instructional leadership or SIT. The data collection tools and templates are meant to aid in the process of data collection, responses, and feedback from students during the 60-second time frame, and in some cases, those tools and templates may serve the full purpose of the One-Minute Meeting for a learning community. There is no harm in going low tech to meet the needs of students; however, school leaders should be intentional in their overall mission and vision for the One-Minute Meeting prior to communicating that message. Courville (2011) stated, "All technology leaders must be wary of the tendency to sacrifice the goals of their position or organization to pursue change for the sake of only innovation and not the proper and effective use of technology." Because the One-Minute Meeting process is in and of itself innovative, the right pieces or programs in technology will only serve to maximize innovation; however, its absence will not sacrifice it. Northhouse (2010) further confirmed this point by asserting, "It is therefore the focus of the leader to ensure that the goal the organization is moving towards is free from any barriers along the path that would interfere in the organization's goal achievement." Allowing technology to convolute the simplicity of the One-Minute Meeting does not move a learning community toward transformation but rather diverts its path and shifts the focus away from authentic interactions with student stakeholders.

Lastly, school leaders must understand that the One-Minute Meeting when implemented to fidelity and with intentionality will change students' overall educational experience. The time spent with each student in the building is a unique window into each of their lives as end users in the process of education, and technology will only enhance that experience if interjected with the same fidelity and intentionality. Fullan (2001) alluded to the moral imperative relevant to educational technology leaders when he purported, "An important end is to make a difference in the lives of students." Being open to the idea that technology may or may not enhance the One-Minute Meeting process will allow school leaders to approach the data analysis and the disaggregation of trends and themes with objectivity and an open mind. The most successful transformation efforts in a learning community are those that do not sacrifice what is right for what is good. Technology is undoubtedly a good thing for the world of education, but if it compromises what is right for students in the span of 60 seconds, then it is not good to include in the One-Minute Meeting process.

One-Minute Challenge:

Data collection and analysis are critical to understanding one's learning community and the changes that are necessary to continue improving it. Because the One-Minute Meeting is a process that is ever evolving, take time to reflect on the data collection tools and templates that the ILT or SIT is using to collect data from the students' responses. Ask the team the following questions:

1. How does the data we are collecting help us reach our school improvement goals?
2. How are we ensuring that the data gleaned from these individual student conferences are positively affecting teaching and learning at our school?
3. How do the overall trends and themes collected from the One-Minute Meeting data compare to other schools in our district, as well as local, state, or nationwide trends?

After answering these questions and discussing them as a team, work to determine implications for improvement of the One-Minute Meeting process. Make necessary revisions, edits, or updates to your data collection tools and templates to continue improving the One-Minute Meeting process for the learning community.

One-Minute Post-Pandemic Strategy

In light of COVID-19, the educational world has embraced digital teaching and learning as a part of the new normal. While each school will be faced with its own particular challenges and situations, school leaders should consider virtual One-Minute Meetings as a part of their initial implementation process. In order to provide students who may be unable to return to regular face-to-face instruction with an opportunity to engage in the process, work to develop virtual office hours to allow them an opportunity to go through the process digitally.

PART 5

THE DATA

Identifying Trends and Themes

One-Minute Reflection Question:
Why is the process of data disaggregation throughout the One-Minute Meeting process so critical to successful school transformation?

In this chapter, school leaders will work intentionally to begin examining and exploring the students' responses to the three big questions during the One-Minute Meeting. Understanding the power of the feedback and how to use it to inform school process, culture, teaching, and learning infuses the One-Minute Meeting into authentic school improvement in any learning environment and serves to amplify students' voices in their own learning journeys. School leaders interact with multiple forms of data on a daily basis from formative and informative assessments, attendance, behavior, and even through regular interactions with students, teachers, and community stakeholders. However, by disaggregating the students' responses to each specific question in the One-Minute Meeting process, school leaders and their leadership teams will be able to identify common trends and themes that are occurring throughout the school and use those findings to significantly affect future instructional practice and processes within the learning community.

> *It says so right here in the data. How can we ignore what the students are telling us?*
> **—A vocal teacher leader and SIT member**

They say that new leaders should never bulldoze their way into organizations. Decades of research urges new leaders, particularly school leaders, to move cautiously as they ease into their new roles, spend time familiarizing themselves with the learning community and its stakeholders, and work to build strong relationships with those stakeholders. As the new leader at FT Elementary, I did not disagree with the research, but the glaring need for change was evident from the failing school letter grade, to the dilapidated culture of the students and teachers, as well as the weak infrastructure of processes and procedures that were gravely affecting teaching and learning. In a school with low morale and even lower achievement scores, I knew within a short amount of time that change was needed—fast.

I had navigated the first few months of leadership with an intense focus on the people. Education is a people business, and without strong, passionate allies, it is nearly impossible to approach the daunting task of transforming a learning community. Our team had listened intently during our preliminary meetings with stakeholders the summer before, and for months after the start of the school year, we observed interactions among students, teachers, and support staff. Our instructional leadership team even researched the content areas that FT Elementary had historically scored well and poorly on to determine if there were any data trends or themes that would help us develop professional development plans for our teacher leaders. Over the past 3 years, FT ELA scores had been on a steady decline, dropping nearly 20% over that course of time. Contrarily, when we pulled the mathematics assessment scores from the same 3-year trend data, FT Elementary exhibited an upward trend of almost 15%, which created a significant gap in overall proficiency for the school.

Our ILT presented the SIT with our findings and began asking some preliminary questions:

1. Were there any notable changes in ELA mandates or instructional programming locally that could account for the decline in scores over the past 3 years?

2. Were there any notable changes in mathematics mandates or instructional programming locally that could account for the increase in scores over the past 3 years?

3. How did focused instructional planning and implementation both in ELA and mathematics affect assessment scores over the past 3 years?

4. How did professional development or the lack thereof affect both ELA and mathematics over the past 3 years?

For over an hour, the team engaged in purposeful discussion and tackled each question from multiple angles. Our teacher leaders attributed the literacy gap to the lack of preparedness when our students started in kindergarten, stating that is difficult to catch them up when they start so far behind. Our support staff spoke to the rising office referrals and mental health referrals that caused students to miss valuable instructional time. Lastly, the ILT criticized the local instructional programming mandates that had changed twice in the past 3 years and stated that the fluctuating expectations in instructional implementation left students and teachers worn out and confused. I watched intently as the team members argued their points passionately, as many of them had worked at FT Elementary for well over 3 years and had seen their share of changes in and throughout the school. It was our reading interventionist, however, who interjected abruptly, capturing everyone's attention when she said, "Y'all I have been at this school for nine years, and I have been in most of your classrooms. Our school serves historically marginalized students who come from poverty. They learn differently and never once have *we* ever been taught how to teach historically marginalized students how to read. Once we learn how to best address their learning needs, the gap will begin to dissolve." Silence.

Following that particular SIT meeting, I headed back to my office worn out and confused myself. Something was causing the gap, but with such diverse opinions and being a new leader, I needed current data to bolster my findings and begin addressing the root cause. The One-Minute Meeting provided a means to obtain current data from current students and possibly insights into the ever-widening achievement gap in ELA and mathematics. After conducting the first round of meetings with our students, our ILT's first initiative was to analyze the responses and compile data specifically on ELA and mathematics. We spent several days compiling our data and disaggregating the major trends before we shared the data with our SIT. Our talented assistant principal color coded the students' responses so that team members could visually compare feedback for both content areas.

When our students referred to their math instruction or math teachers, there was an overwhelming presence of positive affirmations and feelings asserted by our students who used phrases and words such as *"love," "makes learning fun," "comes easy for me,"* and *"brought up my math assessment score this quarter."* When we disaggregated the students' responses regarding literacy, they were compellingly negative with phrases and words such as *"reading is hard," "can't read good," "boring,"* and *"struggled with ELA tests."* The answer was staring us right in the face, straight from the mouths of our students, and before I could suggest that culturally relevant pedagogy was necessary for our learning community, our insightful reading interventionist chimed in saying, "I told y'all we are not reaching our students in reading. It says so right here in the data. How can we ignore what the students are telling us?" As her colleagues nodded in agreement, I smiled to myself. Our students truly held the answers.

The Emotional Compass

School leaders referee a daily battle between their brains and their hearts. Logistically and analytically, school leaders are usually able to navigate the ins and outs of policies and procedures that govern the instruction, operations, and maintenance of a particular learning community. These professional guidelines are often spelled out in handbooks and manuals, enforced by the district office, and governed by local school boards, state boards, or the federal government. But there is a nuance of school leadership that transcends policies and procedures, overlooks the formal methods and, oftentimes, supersedes the regulations—leading from the heart. Conducting the One-Minute Meeting with every student in a learning community will undoubtedly tap into those heartfelt places as one leans in to listen to the challenges and celebrations students are experiencing on a regular basis. It is in this space created by the 60-second process that school transformation is birthed, and it is critical that school leaders position themselves steadily in preparation for the emotional roller coaster that may ensue. Beatty (2007) eloquently described this phenomenon of emotional leadership by stating,

> Holistic school renewal will require a qualitatively different discourse than the current uneasy conversations about school improvement and school effec-tiveness. Leadership for whole school renewal requires emotionally safe spaces

for learning and growing together. Visions of school leadership as distributed, distributive and shared are grounded in notions of collaborative inquiry within dynamic learning communities. For shared leadership to breathe new life into whole school renewal, all leaders, including and especially the principal need to maintain a focus on the moment-to-moment emotional attunements that define experiences in spite of cognitive constructions and beliefs that may coexist alongside of these.

The One-Minute Meeting process provides a portal to organic and authentic change, and on the journey through transformation, school leaders will come face-to-face with their own stereotypes, biases, and assumptions, particularly during data disaggregation. As the school leader imparts the vision of distributive leadership to bring in members of the ILT or SIT to invest minutes and hours with their student stakeholders, there will be crucial conversations about the realities that the student responses reveal. Students will share celebrations that renew leaders' faith in humanity and remind them why they chose education as a profession. Students will divulge challenges that break school leaders' spirits and ignite anger for the circumstances they face. Adult stakeholders and teams involved in the One-Minute Meeting process must equip themselves to navigate through the emotional tumult to remain grounded for the work that is revealed through each student exchange.

Brackett et al. (2018) alluded to the necessity for adequate preparation by asserting, "A recent study found that school leaders who reported greater levels of emotional exhaustion were more likely to experience a range of negative emotions, such as anxiety or anger, and were less likely to experience various positive emotions, such as hope or joy." Learning communities who seek to implement the One-Minute Meeting should be intentional as they prepare to launch the process and allow themselves plenty of time for relaxation, reflection, and self-care before, during, and after implementation. School leaders and their ILTs or SITs are encouraged to point their emotional compasses due north in terms of scheduling classrooms, monitoring hallways during implementation, and even developing time lines to dig into the data rendered from the One-Minute Meetings. Being intentional about creating time and space for relaxation and reflection throughout this process will increase the overall effect of the One-Minute Meeting as a school community and allow adult stakeholders to approach the work with a fresh, energetic perspective.

The One-Minute Meeting process does more than simply allow school stakeholders in a learning community to peer into the dynamic worlds of the most critical stakeholders in the building; it offers a unique opportunity for those adults to model the way for students as well. Patti et al. (2018) asserted that "as school leaders build their leadership self-efficacy, they model their emotional intelligence skills. These leaders actively and regularly articulate their vision to the larger school community." Throughout the One-Minute Meeting process, particularly as teams convene to begin interpreting trends and themes in the data, school leaders who adopt a spirit of transparency and professionalism by articulating their feelings will find that they are creating authentic and safe spaces for other team members to come face-to-face with their emotions. Allow members of the lead instructional team and SIT to grapple with those emotions and create new pathways of learning and healing. Proactive school leaders may plan for the school counselor or mental health liaison to be present during the data meetings, which provides a resource and helpmate on the path to transformation. The One-Minute Meeting is designed to shine a spotlight on the student experience to renew the learning community, but it also provides space to add tools to the toolboxes of the stakeholders charged with leading that renewal.

Disaggregating and Analyzing the Responses

Following the culmination of the One-Minute Meetings in a learning community, it is time to convene the team to disaggregate and analyze the student responses. Depending on the data collection tools and templates employed, school leaders will need to guide their ILT or SIT members to refocus their energies on the needs assessment and mission statement that were developed previously. Take time to review the 3-year trends that emerged after an exhaustive review of the school's instructional, behavioral, socioemotional, and physical data. This will be helpful as teams interpret students' responses and begin to draw out trends and themes in the specific categories. Also revisit the key questions, answers, and outcomes from Chapter 3 that serve as a guide to developing a mission statement for a learning community in transformation. Data disaggregation must be purposeful to glean intentional outcomes, and a school's mission statement and overall school improvement goals should serve as the genesis for data analysis immediately following the One-Minute Meeting.

According to Lewis et al. (n.d.), "A picture may be worth a thousand words, but in education, information speaks volumes. Data analysis can provide a snapshot of what students know, what they should know, and what can be done to meet their academic needs. With appropriate analysis and interpretation of data, educators can make informed decisions that positively affect student outcomes." The One-Minute Meeting provides a new level of information to learning community stakeholders directly from the end users: the students. Their responses to the three specific questions offer a succinct, yet intimate, glimpse into the very type of information that can steer decision-making processes in a holistically student-centered direction. As teams tackle each set of responses, school leaders should encourage team members to adopt a bird's-eye view in the beginning and then drill down in the data based on specific goals. For instance, it is recommended that ILTs or SITs working to disaggregate the data be broken up into various teams: instructional, behavioral, socioemotional, and physical. Each team will then review the 3-year trend data from their specific focus set and then work through the data by grade level, quartile, teacher assignment, or even content area, depending on the data collection tool used to determine trends or themes present in the responses. To guide the thinking and work of the teams' members during this initial phase of data analysis, consider the following data analysis chart that helps teams maximize their work to produce high-quality, positive outcomes for learning communities:

One-Minute Meeting Data Analysis Implementation Guide

Focus Area	Preliminary 3-Year Trend Guiding Questions	Data Analysis Guiding Questions	Keywords or Phrases Associated With Focus Area
Specific area of concentration in student responses	*Questions posed during school needs assessment prior to One-Minute Meeting implementation*	*Questions posed during school needs assessment following One-Minute Meeting implementation*	*Keywords or phrases to look for within student responses*
Instructional (Team One)	Based on our school's needs assessment, what are the areas of celebration in our content data? What are some critical opportunities for improvement in our content data? As we develop our mission statement, which content areas do we want to focus on as a learning community to align our physical, human, and financial resources toward accomplishing that mission? What will be the primary vehicle through which stakeholder groups will increase their impact in those content areas? When will strategic teams analyze content data and create action steps to address opportunities for improvement?	What specific content areas are our students celebrating? What specific instructional strategies are our students celebrating? What specific reasons do students relay when feeling successful in these particular content areas? How do the students' responses to the One-Minute Meeting questions align with our preliminary instructional 3-year trend data? In what content areas do we see discrepancies? In what content areas do we see alignment? How do the students' responses to the One-Minute Meeting questions confirm or refute that we are successfully implementing our mission statement as it relates to instruction for our school? What next steps need to be taken to improve or revise our mission statement as it relates to instruction? Based on students' responses, what opportunities for improvement exist to realign or reassign stakeholder groups to increase their effect on those content areas? What student strengths/ weaknesses does this data highlight? What teacher strengths/ weaknesses does this data highlight? What overall instructional trends or themes are emerging among the data?	English language arts (ELA) Mathematics (Math) Science Social studies Art Physical education (PE) Chorus Band Computer science Business Reading Writing Read aloud Chapters Reading level Homework Solve math problems Learning disability Teamwork Group project Memorize Lecture Technology Figure it out Vocabulary Test Benchmark Assessment College admission Score Report card Progress report Study

(Continued)

One-Minute Meeting Data Analysis Implementation Guide *(Continued)*

Focus Area	Preliminary 3-Year Trend Guiding Questions	Data Analysis Guiding Questions	Keywords or Phrases Associated With Focus Area
Behavioral (Team Two)	Based on our school's needs assessment, what are the areas of celebration in our behavioral data? What are some critical opportunities for improvement in our behavioral data? As we consider our mission statement, what are the key expectations that we want to develop for various stakeholder groups? How will those expectations directly impact desired behaviors in our learning community? What will be the primary vehicle through which stakeholder groups will be introduced to, practice, and measure behavioral expectations in our school? When will strategic teams analyze behavioral data and create action steps to address opportunities for improvement?	What specific behaviors are cited in students' responses as distracting students from learning and teachers from teaching? In what specific locations in the school are students relaying that these behaviors are occurring? What types of professional development will need to be considered for the learning community to address the specific behaviors cited in students' responses? How do the students' responses to the One-Minute Meeting questions confirm or refute that we are successfully implementing our mission statement as it relates to behavior in our school? What next steps need to be taken to improve or revise our mission statement as it relates to instruction or behavior? Based on students' responses, what opportunities for improvement exist to realign or reassign stakeholder groups to increase their effect on behavior in our school? What student strengths/weaknesses does this data highlight? What teacher strengths/weaknesses does this data highlight? What overall behavioral trends or themes are emerging among the data?	Discipline Behavior Behavior chart Rules Cooperative Kind Sharing Sensitive Feelings Fault Blame Trouble Detention Suspension Respect Responsible Safe Expectation Consequences School counselor Mediation Bullying Cyberbullying Social media

(Continued)

One-Minute Meeting Data Analysis Implementation Guide *(Continued)*

Focus Area	Preliminary 3-Year Trend Guiding Questions	Data Analysis Guiding Questions	Keywords or Phrases Associated With Focus Area
Socioemotional (Team Three)	Based on our school's needs assessment, what areas of mental health significantly impact stakeholders in our school?	What specific mental health behaviors are our students citing that are hindering them from learning?	Calm Safe Shy Peaceful Happy Sad Stressed Slone Stressed Overwhelmed Uncomfortable Worried Angry Scared Weird Bullying Cyberbullying Suicide Self-harm Threat School counselor Parents Wellness Self-esteem Emotional Peer pressure Anorexia Bulimia Depression Anxiety Self-harm Mobile crisis Hospital
	What processes currently exist that support our mission as it relates to addressing mental health? Do these processes need to be revisited or redesigned to increase our school's efficacy? If so, how?	What forms of coping and support are our students citing that are available to them in our school? What evidence from the students' responses support that these processes and resources are helpful or hurtful to their overall needs?	
	What processes do not currently exist that we must create to support our mission as it relates to addressing mental health? How will we advocate for, fund, and design these processes to increase our school's efficacy?	How do the students' responses to the One-Minute Meeting questions confirm or refute that we are successfully implementing our mission statement as it relates to mental health in our school?	
		What next steps need to be taken to improve or revise our mission statement as it relates to mental health?	
		Based on students' responses, what opportunities for improvement exist to realign or reassign stakeholder groups to increase their effect on mental health in our school?	
		What student strengths/weaknesses does this data highlight?	
		What teacher strengths/weaknesses does this data highlight?	
		What overall socioemotional trends or themes are emerging among the data?	

(Continued)

One-Minute Meeting Data Analysis Implementation Guide (*Continued*)

Focus Area	Preliminary 3-Year Trend Guiding Questions	Data Analysis Guiding Questions	Keywords or Phrases Associated With Focus Area
Physical (Team Four)	Based on our school's needs assessment, what are the areas of celebration in our physical data and facilities? What are some critical opportunities for improvement in our physical data and facilities? As we consider our mission statement, what physical areas of our school must we focus on improving or redesigning to accomplish our mission? How do we ensure that our physical space and facilities support the ever-changing needs of our school's stakeholder groups? How will we advocate for, fund, and design learning spaces to increase our school's efficacy?	What specific physical areas in our school are our students celebrating? What specific physical areas in our school are our students criticizing? Based on students' responses, what opportunities for improvement exist to redesign or repurpose physical spaces in our school to increase their effect on students' learning experiences? What overall physical trends or themes are emerging among the data?	Classroom Lunchroom Gymnasium (gym) Playground Commons area Computer lab Innovation lab Technology Hallway Bathroom Locker room Sport(s) field(s) Brand new Colorful Run down Does not work Collaborative space Main office Principal's office Bus loading area Car loading area Outdated High tech Connected Plug-in

Thomas (2011) stated, "If educators are going to have a significant, long-term impact on student achievement, we must change the nature of the ongoing work of the adults in a school." School leaders and their ILTs or SITs that commit to the One-Minute Meeting through the data analysis process will begin to experience an undeniable shift in thinking from all stakeholders involved. When students' voices are amplified and adult stakeholders communicate that they are listening, learning communities are unequivocally transformed for the better.

One-Minute Challenge:

School leaders who model the way for their teams are able to develop stronger and more authentic professional relationships throughout the One-Minute Meeting process. Helping school stakeholders tune their emotional compasses during data disaggregation and analysis is an ideal opportunity to model self-care and reflection by devoting the first few minutes of staff meetings, school improvement meetings, or team meetings to quiet reflection and meditation. Before beginning the meeting, remind teacher leaders and team members how valuable their knowledge, expertise, and input are to the process of school transformation. Then inform stakeholders that the entire group is going to take a few minutes to simply breathe, participate in quiet reflection, or simply close their eyes for a brief moment to gain clarity. Encourage all stakeholders to silence their phones and alert the front office staff to hold all calls and announcements. Start the timer and set it for 1, 3, or 5 minutes. Once the timer goes off, remind stakeholders that we have to be intentional in caring for our bodies, as well as our minds, to ensure that our students get the benefits of our best selves throughout the school year!

One-Minute Post-Pandemic Strategy

The impact of the pandemic has caused incredible angst and anxiety in our students, teacher leaders, school stakeholders, and school leaders! Academic research has shown that meditation and mindfulness has had positive effects in addressing the rising levels of undesirable behavior and mental health needs of school stakeholders. As you work to redesign the approach to teaching and learning, discuss the option of introducing school-wide meditation and mindfulness as a way to start or end the school day with your ILT and school improvement team. Being proactive about addressing immediate post-pandemic needs will greatly reduce anxiety in your learning community!

Implementing and Sustaining Change

One-Minute Reflection Question:
How can school leaders use the One-Minute Meeting data trends and themes to implement and sustain transformational change in teaching and learning?

In this chapter, school leaders will use the trends and themes extrapolated from the One-Minute Meetings in their learning communities and begin to implement intentional changes in teaching and learning. Disaggregating the students' responses provides a transformational road map for school leaders and their instructional lead or SITs. Understanding where to begin with implementing change in policy, practice, and pedagogy requires planning, time, and patience for the changes to be not only well received but also thoroughly understood by students, teacher leaders, and school stakeholders. Implementing and sustaining change in a transformational learning community requires a team of change agents who are immersed in the One-Minute Meeting process from beginning to end. When led by a school leader who is able to create productive and safe spaces for innovation and exploration, the learning community benefits from the process of continuous improvement.

> *Never in my sixteen-year career have I had permission to do it that way.*
> **—An enlightened and relieved veteran teacher leader**

The results were in, and our ILT stood at the whiteboard in the PLC room with smiles on our faces and hope in our hearts. We had asked our students to tell us about FT Elementary, and they did not disappoint. With less than 4 months before EOG exams, our ILT had committed to being strategic and intentional in our efforts to support our student stakeholders and their teacher leaders to create a culture of productive failure in our transforming learning community. Being deemed an "F" school by the state was a tough pill to swallow, and since the start of school in August, we had been as forthcoming and transparent as possible in relation to the changes that were desperately needed at FT Elementary. From the Walmart conversations to help our school stakeholders tackle tough conversations in the community about our school to approaching our mission and vision with fidelity on all levels, the One-Minute Meeting data analysis provided the missing piece to our ever-evolving and changing puzzle.

All of the students had provided critical feedback that would help us improve practice and policy from kindergarten through fifth grade; however, our upper-grade students offered us fresh insight and perspective that we truly had not considered before. Based on the third and final question of the One-Minute Meeting process—*What challenges or concerns are you experiencing in your class(es) or in our school?*—the instructional data showed that a significant number of students were struggling in either ELA or mathematics because of the time of day in which core instruction was delivered. Similarly, the behavioral data also pointed to a considerable uptick in discipline referrals (thus leading to lost instructional time) in the afternoons following lunch. Our instructional facilitator was the first to recognize this correlation once we aligned the third-, fourth-, and fifth-grade data, we noticed that this was a trend that affected all of the tested grades. We knew that small changes in the master schedule would help to address our students' instructional needs; however, altering the master schedule in the fourth quarter in elementary school was similar to switching your starting quarterback for your third string in the fourth quarter of the Super Bowl. If we wanted to infuse our students' voices and needs into informing our practice, we needed to ensure that our SITs, grade-level chairs, and teacher leaders were able to fully maximize *their* voices and expertise to make this modification happen while still sustaining our momentum.

To maximize our next SIT meeting, our ILT sent the entire team the data trends and themes prior to the meeting. In the email, we provided our teacher leaders and support staff with easy-to-read and easy-to-interpret data charts by grade level that would assist them in understanding the student feedback. We also asked that they take 10 to 15 minutes to look over the data prior to the meeting and be prepared to share initial thoughts and takeaways at the start of the meeting. After a long day of teaching and learning, we recognized that it was sometimes difficult for school stakeholders to wrap their minds around data, so we wanted to provide a fresh mental landscape to maintain the integrity of the data and the process of implementing key changes to our learning community. After sending the email, I tasked our instructional facilitator, our assistant principal, and myself with having face-to-face conversations with the grade-level chairs for third, fourth, and fifth grade to front-load them with our initial findings. Conversations, not checklists, grow leaders, and we respected our teacher leaders as professionals, so we wanted them to be armed with as much information and insight as possible since the bulk of the meeting would be focused on these upper grades. On the day of the meeting, everyone arrived with data either in hand or on their school laptops, and I opened the discussion by thanking everyone for their hard work thus far this school year and opened the floor for comments, questions, and/or concerns regarding the One-Minute Meeting data.

During the first round of the One-Minute Meetings at FT Elementary, I worked to model the way and had taken the lead in not only conducting the meetings but also disaggregating the data and presenting the results. During this third rendition, however, the efficacy of the students and teachers was increasing, and the One-Minute Meeting process was a welcome entity in our everyday transformational discussions. One by one, our teacher leaders and support staff expressed that they were humbled by the students' responses. The school counselor stated that she was seeing a difference during group lessons in how students addressed not only one another but also adults in the building. She said that the data showed students had a better handle on their emotions, and those who were still struggling knew the appropriate language to articulate their feelings. The first- and second-grade teacher leaders pointed out that the data showed students were celebrating literacy and reading, which was a testament to the carefully designed mission goals that we had committed to at FT Elementary. Finally, our third-grade teacher leader interjected: "We have been struggling for years with math and ELA scores for our students. Every two or three years the scores fluctuate. With changing instructional programs, changing schedules, and changing administration, it has been hard to pinpoint the exact problem, but the data this year says that students are struggling with math in the afternoons. Dr. Hemphill, I know we talked, and you asked for me to reflect on how my class is affected, and the students are so sluggish and tired after lunch that I am having a hard time motivating them to focus on these math concepts. What can we do?" While she was relaying her thoughts, I could see out of the corner of my eye the fourth- and fifth-grade teacher leaders nodding in agreement.

We were arming our teacher leaders with the very thing that we wanted for our student leaders: opportunity and space to create and implement change. Following our third-grade teacher leaders' observations, the entire SIT began analyzing the upper grades' master schedule. After about an hour of discussion, data alignment, and resource allocation, the team determined that offering mathematics and ELA on an alternating schedule for the fourth quarter would not only meet the needs of students who were struggling with either ELA or mathematics instruction in the afternoon but also provide the perfect opportunity for review in the weeks leading up the EOG exams. As we worked to ensure that all students would still receive their pullouts for exceptional or academically gifted services despite the schedule changes, the third-grade teacher leader pulled me aside and said, "Dr. Hemphill, like I mentioned, I have been struggling for years to figure out how to address the afternoon slump with my students. Never in my sixteen-year career have I had permission to do it that way. For the first time in my career, I am excited about EOG exams because I know my students will actually have a chance to be successful. Thank you." Before I offered my thanks for this teacher's boldness, willingness to change, and overall insight into what is truly best for the students, I paused. Our students were helping us grow. In a way, they were becoming the best teachers our teachers had ever had.

SITs and ILTs

According to Gunn (2018), "Transformational leadership in schools is when a leader empowers members of the learning community to improve from within. The transformational leader does not simply run a school, merely keeping it afloat. Instead, such leaders seek to make things better through genuine collaboration between the school's members and stakeholders." For decades, the model of education has focused on a top-down approach that focuses on the school leader as the sole owner of knowledge, the sole creator of instructional design and implementation, and the sole owner of accolades associated with transformational change. The One-Minute Meeting shatters that notion and levels the landscape for all school stakeholders to not only have an equal and equitable voice in the process of change but also equal and equitable opportunities to grow as thinkers and leaders. Throughout the process of data disaggregation and analysis with SITs and ILTs, it is critical for school leaders to include all members of the team in the process of decision making, as well as laying the groundwork for change. As SITs begin to experience how to approach problems of practice and observe the school leader modeling change through the One-Minute Meeting, it will invite members into a space that elevates them as professionals and experts in the educational space. Munger and von Frank (2010) alluded to this need, stating, "School leadership teams are based on the understanding that change is needed, change must occur at the school level, and school leaders create understanding of change and a sense of urgency and purpose for it." By undergirding the urgency that is necessary for the learning community in transition, as well as the purpose for change with current student feedback and critical school data, school leaders are able to build professional capacity in their teams. The One-Minute Meeting process leverages positional power by demonstrating the need for everyone's knowledge, expertise, and perspective to move a school toward its overall goals of success.

The ILT serves as a major catalyst for change when it comes to the One-Minute Meeting in that it lays the foundation upon which understanding, implementation, and communication are built for learning communities. School leaders who choose to pursue this course of action should sit down with their ILT members and have candid conversations about the need for the One-Minute Meeting as a whole and the potential impact for change *before* making plans to begin. Munger and von Frank (2010) went on to express that

> principals have a critical role in developing the leadership team members' abilities. To be able to develop capacity in individual learning teams, leadership team members need guidance on their roles, responsibilities, effective meetings, and understanding change and its impact. The job of finding ways to improve instruction to better meet students' needs then rests with the team.

The ILT has a substantial amount of interaction with key stakeholders, both internally and externally. Ensuring that they fully understand the why behind the One-Minute Meeting better equips them to respond to questions from teacher leaders and school support staff; assists them in addressing questions and concerns from parents, guardians, and community stakeholders; and, ultimately, elevates their awareness on how to implement and sustain schoolwide change. Having key conversations and check-ins from inception all the way to implementation significantly increases opportunities for success for all stakeholders and ensures a more seamless transformation throughout the school year.

To avoid simply executing the One-Minute Meeting at the surface level, creating conditions for sustainability is critical as well. Oftentimes, schools that are in need of transformation experience high levels of turnover of teacher and school leaders, are met with a lack of human and fiscal capital, and, unfortunately, suffer from low to commensurable school morale. These types of circumstances can make sustaining a transformative process such as the One-Minute Meeting especially difficult for student stakeholders who may be met with varying behavioral expectations, disparate instructional targets, and even unfamiliar socioemotional experiences throughout the turnover. Whether a beginning school leader or a veteran, identifying the area of greatest need for the learning community and aligning that need to the overall mission and school improvement goals provides direction for the One-Minute Meeting transformative process. SIT and ILT members who navigate through the needs assessment, one-on-one student meetings, data disaggregation, and implementation with that area in mind will experience the far-reaching effects of their leadership from the classroom to the community.

Individual Teacher Leaders

The One-Minute Meeting process will be a novel undertaking for many schools and their stakeholders; however, teacher leader feedback throughout the process provides school leaders, SITs, and ILTs with valuable perceptions and observations that will help the learning community avoid critical pitfalls and setbacks. Shifting the paradigm of positional power with the One-Minute Meeting process shifts the traditional power of the school administrator equally and equitably to each stakeholder who directly or indirectly affects students' experiences and learning outcomes. With innovative educational ideas always comes skepticism, inquiry, and doubt; however, school leaders who organically involve teacher leaders will find that the process is much more engaging and empowering for all involved. Gunn (2018) argued, "School leaders and teachers often rely on tried and true practices that may be comfortable, but ineffective. To truly transform a community we must question and sometimes abandon habits, beliefs, practices, and mindsets that no longer work."

There will be those teacher leaders who embrace the One-Minute Meeting process as an important shift in school vision, culture, and practice. These teacher leaders often are the first to adopt the process and differentiate it to meet the needs of students in their own classrooms, and they also advocate for the student-centered practice among their colleagues. There will be those teacher leaders, however, who are hesitant to support the practice and doubt the validity of student feedback, even after they have observed a few rounds being conducted and analyzed the data themselves. PLCs, grade-level and department chairs, as well as SIT members, are prime resources to interact with the latter group of teacher leaders who will need consistent communication regarding the process, irrefutable data that demonstrates a positive shift in teaching and learning, and anecdotal data from their colleagues to eventually embrace the One-Minute Meeting as an impetus for change. Teacher leadership serves as the lynchpin for success in the One-Minute Meeting process. Because teacher leaders log the most contact hours with student stakeholders, school leaders who are able to develop teacher leaders in the learning community through distributive leadership will see sustainable impact throughout the school's transformation. Teacher leadership speaks not only to the essence of developing and carrying out a shared vision within a school but also promotes teachers as critical players in the development of thriving learning communities. The key role that teacher leaders play in executing specific changes to practice, policy, and pedagogy based on students' feedback during the One-Minute Meetings works to transform learning communities authentically and holistically with students in mind.

Parents/Guardians, and Community Stakeholders

External stakeholders possess a unique perspective and can provide crucial insight into the One-Minute Meeting process given the right opportunities. Parents, guardians, and community stakeholders who are genuinely invested in the transformation of a learning community typically have a special connection to the school either through their own children, family members, or neighborhood interests. These stakeholders can serve as ambassadors for the learning community and champions of the One-Minute Meeting process provided they are well informed about how the process specifically affects teaching and learning, culture and morale, and parental and community involvement. Sheldon and Epstein (2002) argued,

> The leadership determines the culture of the school and the school culture is the rhythm of what parents, students and teachers follow. It is imperative to have a leader that believes in creating support networks with parents in place. Researchers believe that creating communication from the school to home via academics, giving parenting advice for the home, parental volunteering within the school, teaching parents how to help their children with their homework, including parents in school decision making and creating community partnerships are successful attributes in creating a positive school culture to curtail negative behavior.

School leaders must be willing and able to develop authentic relationships between families and community stakeholders and the learning community. As a bridge builder, the school leader will be able to use the relationships built and increase impact with the One-Minute Meeting process. When these stakeholders grasp the purpose of the One-Minute Meeting as a vehicle for change that focuses on students' experiences and feedback to inform pedagogy, practice, and policy for positive change, there is no doubt that they will be willing to support, assist, and volunteer as needed. Green (2015) further illustrated this point by stating, "It is about making valuable connections with the community, especially the parents. When a school has the support of the parents, then the child will be a success and the classroom teacher will be free to revolutionize the student mind." Creating a structured system of communication and maintaining an open-door policy for parents/guardians and community stakeholders leads to effective change that has long-lasting effects.

One-Minute Challenge:

Gathering external feedback provides school leaders with an up-to-date pulse on how the school is perceived in the community, as well as among parents/guardians and families. Creating opportunities for these critical stakeholders to share their feedback also opens the door for school leaders and their ILT to arm these groups with information about the school, correct erroneous messages or data, and dispel myths or rumors that may be circulating about the school overall. Work with the ILT on the morning and afternoon duty schedules to provide coverage for members of the SIT to cover car rider duty during those times. Arrange to arrive for car rider duty a few minutes early to catch those parents who are dropping off late or picking them up early and ask if you can have 1 minute to informally survey them about their child's and their own experiences with your school. Develop no more than two questions that are strategically focused on your school's greatest need and that align with the school's mission statement and school improvement goals. Collect the stakeholders' responses and feedback and share with the ILT and SIT to further inform the next steps, alongside the One-Minute Meeting data and student responses.

One-Minute Post-Pandemic Strategy

COVID-19 elevated the need for schools, students, parents, and families to have a strong relationship centered around students' success and sustainability. As virtual and blended learning and communication become preferred modes of teaching and reaching all school stakeholders, extend these communication options to parents and families as well. Utilizing social media or alternative digital forms of communication in a safe and confidential way is a highly effective way of maintaining an open-door policy to keep school stakeholders connected to their students' support systems.

Balancing Transformation and Testing

One-Minute Reflection Question:
What are the necessary steps for school leaders to develop learning communities where transformation and testing thrive in harmony?

In this chapter, school leaders will address the industry-old adage, "teaching to the test." For decades, public education has been embroiled with the ideology that student leaders and teacher leaders embark on a journey that leads only to how well they both perform on a standardized test. The One-Minute Meeting introduces a process for change that challenges the notion of traditional teaching and learning and instead invites all stakeholders in the learning community to embark on a transformational process that cannot be defined or embodied by a single test. To balance reframing change against the traditional stagnant testing culture, school leaders must develop a healthy community of productive failure that allows teacher leaders to dive deeply into innovation in their pedagogical practice and student stakeholders to stand proudly on their unique talents, skills, and gifts. School leaders who are able to nurture that capacity in all the key stakeholders within the learning community will find that using the One-Minute Meeting for student-centered transformation takes care of the testing altogether.

I do not want you to focus on being a Level 1, 2, 3, or 4.
I want you to focus on what you know you know.
— **Dr. Hemphill to the students on the day of EOG exams**

It was exactly 1 year since I started at FT Elementary, and what a year it had been! From changing the Walmart conversation about our school to tackling the process of developing a new mission statement and not to mention the implementation of the One-Minute

Meeting with every student in our building, I could not have been prouder of our students, teacher leaders, support staff, and community for rallying together! The much-needed transformation and instructional shifts were still in process, and we were morphing FT Elementary into the best place to work and learn in the district. Even without a tangible instrument to measure the change in culture, however, there was substantial evidence that our school community was headed in the right direction. I was sitting at my desk looking at projected enrollment for the school year ahead and noticed an increase of almost 25 students from the year before. As had been the norm for FT Elementary before this past school year, parents and guardians did all they could to ensure that their children who were assigned to our zone submitted a waiver to go to another elementary school in the district or they went so far as to move out of the district altogether. But with lots of hard work and dedication by our incredible school family and community stakeholders, the buzz was that FT Elementary was on its way to rewriting the rumors of being a failing school and that children were learning and thriving in our building!

This revelation came on the heels of even more amazing news from the week prior. Following a district principal's meeting, the director of human resources asked each school leader to stop by his office to pick up their transfer forms and materials. Prior to the end of each school year, principals in our school system received a list of those teacher leaders and support staff members who requested a transfer to another school or position within the district. School leaders had a window during which they could recruit; however, all transfers had to be agreed upon by both the receiving and sending principal and, of course, human resources had to sign off. I was the last in line to receive my packet, and when I reached in the basket for the envelope labeled "FT Elementary," the receptionist squealed with excitement and yelled, "Congratulations!"

Surprised at her elation, I looked around to determine who she might have been congratulating only to find that we were the only two in the office. "What are you congratulating me for?" I asked with bewilderment.

She replied, "Dr. Hemphill, your school had no transfer requests for the first time ever! I am hearing great things about your school, so, of course, no one wants to leave!" Stunned, I grabbed the folder, thanked the receptionist for her help and the kind words, and ran down the hallway to get back to school to share the news with our ILT. One hundred percent retention?! FT Elementary would have the amazing opportunity to begin the new school year with the same cadre of individuals who had helped to begin this transformation, and, more importantly, our students would be returning to familiar faces, expectations, and passions, which for a school in transition was critical to its sustained success.

Summer was a sacred time for school leaders. While much of the world envied teachers and principals who were "lucky" to have summers off and realistically believed that students around the world arrive on the first day of school to a magically operable school, summers were my busiest time. With the hot summer months now upon us, I got up from my desk to adjust the thermostat that controlled both our assistant principal's office and mine. After I lowered the air conditioning a few degrees, the doorbell rang, and I made my way through the front office to press the camera buzzer for the front door. As soon as I heard the click of the security lock, one of my awesome third-grade scholars, Toni, ran through the front office door and almost tripped over herself to give me a hug. Toni's mother just laughed and picked Toni's sweet baby sister up from her stroller so that I could see how much she had grown since the last time they visited.

"She has gotten so big!" I exclaimed.

"Yes, she has," Toni's mother replied, "and she is just as bright as her sister!"

I gave Toni a high five and a wink for being an amazing help to her mother. "What can I help you with today?" I asked.

Toni's mother informed me that they had moved right after the end of the school year and wanted to stop by to get Toni's report card. The school district sent all fourth-quarter report cards home, along with the EOG score reports for students. Students and their families enjoyed getting the fourth-quarter report cards because they loved seeing the culminating statement: *Your student is promoted to the next grade level.* Our data manager kept a mail bin near her desk for all report cards that were returned because of incorrect addresses, and I quickly located Toni's name and handed her mother the envelope.

She passed the envelope to Toni and said, "I will let her do the honors. She has worked so hard!"

Toni excitedly took the envelope and plopped down in one of the new oversized chairs in our front lobby. As she slid the thick stack of papers from their holder, I could tell that she was anxious. She unfolded her report card, and I watched affectionately as her eyes went from the top grade to the final grade, and then she screamed, "I PASSED THIRD GRADE!" At this point, her volume and excitement startled her baby sister, and in her mother's flustered state, I offered to hold the baby while she properly hugged and congratulated her new fourth-grade daughter.

After squeezing her mother's neck, Toni then reached for the EOG score reports: one for ELA and the other for mathematics. As soon as she was able to calm herself long enough to comprehend them, she squealed again, screaming, "I PASSED BOTH EOGS WITH FOURS!"

At this point, Toni's mother had tears in her eyes, and I was beginning to tear up myself. This student was experiencing the pure joy of hard work, dedication, and success, and I was honored to know that our devoted team had played a part in her story.

Toni hugged her mother again, and then jumped off the chair and ran over to me, grabbing a hold of my waist. "Thank you, Dr. Hemphill!" she said.

"No thank *you*, Toni. You worked hard, you focused, and you set your goals and achieved them. I am so proud of you." I replied.

"But Dr. Hemphill," she said, "it's just like you said on the intercom the day of the exam. Do not focus on being a Level 1, 2, 3, or 4. Focus on what you know you know, and that's what I did!"

Toni did focus on that and so did many of her fellow classmates and friends at FT Elementary. As I carefully placed Toni's little sister back in the stroller, the doorbell rang again. I reached over the counter to press the buzzer, and our district's assistant superintendent of curriculum and instruction came prancing in. After telling Toni and her family to have an amazing and restful summer, our assistant superintendent handed me a folded piece of paper with a smile on her face. I slowly opened the paper, and it said,

FT Elementary

Projected Letter Grade: D

Projected Growth: 86.7%

Growth Index: Exceeds

We had increased a whole letter grade and exceeded growth! The "F" was gone! Our students had helped us to change trajectories, and we were only going up from here.

It Is a Process

School improvement is an ever-evolving cycle of continuous improvement. When this process occurs within learning communities that have experienced significant difficulties in the past, it makes that process even more arduous because of the layers of obstacles the school leader must guide school stakeholders through successfully. From human capital to financial capital and culture to community, underperforming schools present a unique set of barriers that require an innovative, courageous, and transformational school leader to champion the charge. Denmark (2012) supported this notion by stating, "Staying true to research, for transformation to occur in an underperforming school or school system, then leaders must act as system thinkers. True transformation happens not in silo-structured organizations, but in organizations that respect all of their elements, maintain their interconnectedness, and have a common purpose." While schools in need of transformation are not always underperforming, they do present specific areas of need and attention that can be determined through completing the detailed and critical needs assessment. Despite the outcomes and analysis, no learning community can accomplish full-scale, sustainable change without maximizing and empowering all stakeholders from the students to the adult stakeholders that support them. Schoolwide transformation requires a system that is flexible enough to account for the uncontrolled variables that manifest throughout the school year (i.e., curricular changes, federal/state/local mandates and legislation, personnel changes, natural disasters, etc.) and the controlled ones (i.e., budget allocations, state-mandated testing, building operations, etc.). Despite the ebb and flow of these variables throughout the journey, transformational school leaders understand that transformation is a process.

Implementation of the One-Minute Meeting is one means of codifying systemic change within a learning community that maximizes the roles, voices, and experiences of all school stakeholders and provides multiple pathways to effectual change. The One-Minute Meeting process will look different within each learning community based on the specific needs of the school and school stakeholders themselves; however, it is within the process that the power to affect change is equally realized. Yang (2013) eloquently described this power sharing during school transformation by asserting,

> Sharing power is the opportunity to school improvement. Sharing power means returning the power to the school members, what's more, it means the principal's higher expectation to the members, and he believes everyone is an excellent leader. This indicates that sharing power means trust and respect, and it is the best way to encourage the members. School improvement is a step-by-step process, if we don't have enough accumulation, we won't achieve transcendence success. So, school development is each teacher and student's duty and they should work hard together. When every member participates in school management

positively, the school will have a foundation of teamwork, and then the higher school efficacy become possible. Therefore, the essence of the power sharing is to stimulate the enthusiasm of the members, to develop their potential and to promote school development.

Transformation cannot occur without enthusiasm from the school stakeholders who are responsible for students' learning. As school leaders work to share their perceived power, they will find that some individuals are unable to perform, some individuals will not rise to the occasion, and some individuals will misuse their opportunities to lead. This is part of the process and helps the school leader to better hone her/his skills in determining who key players are and what is expected of them. The beauty of transformation is that for every individual who seems to derail the process or slow it down even slightly, there is an individual in the learning community who will exceed the school leaders' expectations, surprise the entire school with untapped potential, and emerge as a catalyst for change despite their past experiences in their current role. These are the moments when sustainable change for teaching and learning is realized, and these are the moments that school leaders must lean into when creating systemic change in the midst of an era that is defined by standardized testing, data, and student achievement.

Productive Failure

In the 21st century, it is pivotal that school leaders design learning communities that allow for all its stakeholders to fail productively. With the amount of, and access to, technology and digital data increasing exponentially on a daily basis, society, employers, and communities require citizens, employees, and change agents who know how to fail forward armed with unparalleled perseverance, grit, and tenacity. Kageyama (2019) described the goals of productive failure as follows: "So in much the way that spaced, random, and variable practice lead to worse performance in the short term, but better performance in the long term, it seems that the goal of productive failure is not to get the correct answer via shallower learning ('unproductive success'), but instead, to cultivate a deeper understanding of the fundamental principles and various ways of arriving at a solution regardless of short-term performance." To lead schools full of digital natives who have access to the World Wide Web of information, opportunities, and billions of people, school leaders have an obligation to instill urgency in their ILTs and SITs in regard to creating safe spaces for students and teacher leaders to fail productively. When students set goals for themselves during the One-Minute Meeting, they are manifesting attainable verbal and mental models of success for themselves. School stakeholders are charged with developing conditions that help students achieve these goals whether instructionally, behaviorally, or emotionally and all must be prepared should a student not reach their goals. Student leaders should be able to observe their teachers' failures, ask critical questions of themselves and others, develop a course of action to address the missteps, and step back into the action of pursuing success. The One-Minute Meeting process brings students, school leaders, teacher leaders, and support staff face-to-face with the processes, policies, and pedagogies that have been failing schools for decades and offers an opportunity to reimagine and reimage them into productive practices that transform learning communities with students at the forefront.

Kageyama (2019) went on to purport that "it seems that the productive failure approach also increases engagement in the learning process." One of the biggest proponents of transformational success in a learning community is that school stakeholders observe productive failure as active engagement and active death by fire. As most school leaders navigate the delicate balance of innovation and standardized testing alongside local politics and community obligation, when all school stakeholders feel genuinely engaged in their own growth, it makes failure all the more palpable for the learning community. The more opportunities school leaders provide for school stakeholders, particularly for student stakeholders through the One-Minute Meeting process, the more opportunities stakeholders have to succeed or productively fail. The One-Minute Meeting inventories students' perceptions of their opportunities and how stakeholders in the school are responding to and adjusting accordingly. When growth and change are approached through the eyes of the end users—the students—then school leaders have firm ground to stand on in determining capacities and capital in developing a system of change that achieves all school goals and manifests the school's mission.

There are questions school leaders can ask and reflect on to determine whether their learning community cultivates a community of stakeholders who are failing productively:

- How often are teacher leaders intentionally providing learning opportunities that stretch students' thinking beyond rote memorization?

- How do school stakeholders respond to student leaders and one another when someone fails (i.e., gets an answer wrong, does poorly on a test/exam, teaches an incorrect process, etc.)?

- How do student leaders respond to one another when one of their classmates fails (i.e., gets an answer wrong, does poorly on a test/exam, performs poorly in public, etc.)

- How quickly do student leaders recover from their public failures?

- How quickly do teacher leaders and support staff recover from their public failures?

- How do school stakeholders describe their failures to others (i.e., "the end of the world," "mortifying," "learning opportunities," "not a big deal," etc.)?

- Are students incorporating their failures into their plan of action during the One-Minute Meeting (i.e., academic goal setting, behavioral goal setting, emotional goal setting, etc.)?

The answers and findings to these strategic questions will allow school leaders to develop a true portrait of whether their learning communities are equipped to produce students and school stakeholders who embrace or reject productive failure. With high-stakes testing at the forefront of a majority of conversations in public education, productive failure helps learning communities celebrate small wins on the path to huge accomplishments. Productive failure buffers the release of test scores publicly to community stakeholders who sometimes do not understand the big picture. Productive failure serves as a vehicle for veteran teachers who are adjusting their instructional practices for the first time in years based on student feedback from the One-Minute Meetings. Finally, productive failure supports school leaders to understand that even with what seems like an airtight system, transformation manifests in the most unexpected ways and at the most unexpected times. Embracing the failures, along with the improvements, is the only way to navigate the journey of school improvement.

It's All About the People

Education is a people business, and it is about how big people help little people become the best big people they can possibly be. There is a motto in education that says, "Meet the students where they are." While this is an extremely appropriate directive, it does not provide any instructions for what to do after we come face-to-face with our most important clients in education: our students. Public education asks so much of students and the stakeholders charged with their education. The traditional model of schools requires that they stand in straight lines, sit in straight rows, bubble in perfect ovals, and learn facts and information in the correct sequence when the reality of the 21st century is that life does not happen in a straight line, nothing and no one is perfect, and rarely if ever does it happen in a correct sequence of events. School leaders who are charged with transforming learning communities must find ways to deeply and organically infuse the people into the process, and the One-Minute Meeting puts the people—students—at the center of that process.

When school leaders lead with the people in mind—not the pedagogy, the policy, or the instructional practices—the testing fades into the background because learning communities begin producing problem solvers and solution seekers who can think critically and reflect thoroughly on their individual experiences and pathways. The One-Minute Meeting process raises the volume on the voices of students and asks how they perceive the learning environment designed for their overall success. The process then uses their feedback to inform critical challenges and celebrations in how the school operates and functions as a whole, all while providing teacher leaders and support staff with an in-depth look at how they have the ability to change and govern that path to change. Student leaders and teacher leaders who engage with transformation at this level undoubtedly approach the process of teaching and learning with renewed fervor and an unbridled appreciation for the process. The real world will never ask students what they made on their fifth-grade science exam or their seventh-grade math assessment or their eleventh-grade advanced placement calculus test. The real world will, however, ask our students how they overcame their struggles with test anxiety, how they became so good with doing math and crunching numbers in their heads, or how they landed the job over the other qualified candidates because they decided never to give up on their goals. School leaders have a unique opportunity to shift how school is done by placing students in their rightful place in education—at the center—where they belong and where they deserve to be to ensure that school transformation continues long into the 22nd century.

One-Minute Challenge:

Developing a culture of productive failure requires consistent dedication and analysis to determine key areas of development in a learning community. School leaders must first determine the current climate to create a strategic plan that allows all school stakeholders to have the necessary tools to productively fail. Along with the ILT, school leaders should choose five key stakeholders in the learning community: (1) a student leader, (2) a teacher leader, (3) a support staff/personnel member, (4) a community stakeholder, (5) and a parent/guardian/family member. Using the questions outlined in the "Productive Failure" section of this chapter, choose the appropriate questions for each stakeholder and take a minute or two to informally pose the questions. Collect the responses and come together as an ILT to analyze the results. Share the findings and outcomes with the SIT team to begin brainstorming what your learning community can do in the short and long term to ensure that your school breeds productive failure.

One-Minute Post-Pandemic Strategy

As one of many challenges and barriers highlighted by this recent pandemic, assessing student learning has become a topic of widespread discussion among school leaders across the country. While traditional grading and testing has provided the backdrop for student accountability for decades, post-pandemic teaching and learning provides an excellent opportunity for school leaders to pave the way in thinking innovatively about the role of alternative student assessment. Work with your ILT and school improvement team to discuss effective new ways to assess students' learning including academic portfolios, performance-based assessments, and digital assessments. Diversifying the manner in which schools approach assessment is one way to pave the way to post-pandemic success for all students!

REFERENCES

Argyris, C., & Schon, D. (1978). *Organizational learning: A theory of action perspective.* Reading, MA: Addison-Wesley.

Allison, D. J. (1981). Public schools and Weberian bureaucracy: A summary [PDF]. *Education Resources Information Center.* Retrieved from https://files.eric.ed.gov/fulltext/ED235581.pdf

Anderson, A. et al. (1999). At issue: Improving the perception of public education. Retrieved from http://horizon.unc.edu/projects/issues/papers/Anderson.html

Arter, J. A. (2013). Assessment for learning: Classroom assessment to improve student achievement and well-being [PDF]. *Educational Resources Information Center,* 463–484. Retrieved from https://files.eric.ed.gov/fulltext/ED480068.pdf

Austin, S., Anderson-Davis, D., Graham, J., & White, M. (2018). Instructional leadership teams to the rescue. NASSP. https://www.nassp.org/2018/09/01/instructional-leadership-teams-to-the-rescue/

Bear, G. G. (2010). Self-discipline and the social and emotional learning approach to school discipline. *School Discipline and Self Discipline*: A *Practical Guide to Promoting Prosocial Student Behavior,* 37–54. Retrieved from http://apps.nasponline.org/resources-and-publications/books-and-products/samples/HCHS3_Samples/S4H18_Discipline.pdf

Bagshaw, M. (2009). Innocents abroad in the new millennium: How well does the American leadership model travel? *Global Leadership: Portraits of the Past, Visions for the Future,* 51–64.

Beatty, B. (2007). Going through the emotions: Leadership that gets to the heart of school renewal. *Australian Journal of Education,* 51(3). https://doi.org/10.1177%2F000494410705100309

Blase, J., & Blase, J. (2006). *Teachers bringing out the best in teachers: A guide to peer consultation for administrators and teachers.* Thousand Oaks, CA: Corwin Press.

Brackett, M. A., Floman, J. L., & Bradley, C. (2018). *Emotion revolution for education leaders (survey).* [Unpublished data]. Yale University.

Bragg, S. & Fielding, M. (2003). *Students as researchers: Making a difference.* London, UK: Pearson Publishers.

Buchanan, R., Nese, R. N., & Clark, M. (2016). Stakeholders' voices: Defining needs of students with emotional and behavioral disorders transitioning between school settings. *Behavioral Disorders,* 41(3), 135–147. https://www.ncbi.nlm.nih.gov/pmc/articles/PMC5916839/

Burkhauser, S. Gates, S. M., Hamilton, L. S., & Ikemoto, G. S. (2012) First-year principals in urban school districts: How actions and working conditions relate to outcomes. *RAND Corporation.* Retrieved from https://www.rand.org/pubs/technical_reports/TR1191.html

Campbell, P. (2015). Why you should celebrate everything. *Psychology Today.* https://www.psychologytoday.com/us/blog/imperfect-spirituality/201512/why-you-should-celebrate-everything

Courville, K. (2011, November 28–29). *Educational technology: Effective leadership and current initiatives* [Paper presentation]. Louisiana Computer Using Educator's Conference, New Orleans, LA, United States. https://files.eric.ed.gov/fulltext/ED527339.pdf

Covey, S. R. (2005). *The 8th habit: From effectiveness to greatness.* New York: Free Press.

Deal, T., & Peterson, K. (1999). *Shaping school culture: The heart of leadership* (2nd ed). San Francisco, CA: Jossey-Bass.

Delisio, E. R. (2008). Easy ways to market your schools. *Education World.* Retrieved from https://www.educationworld.com/a_admin/admin/admin384.shtml

Denmark V. (2012). Transformational leadership—a matter of perspective. Source. https://www.advanced.org/source/transformational-leadership-matter-perspective

Dewey, J. (1915). *The school and society.* Chicago, IL: University of Chicago Press.

Dewey, J. (1916). *Democracy and education: An introduction to the philosophy of education. New* York: Macmillan.

DuFour, R., & Eaker, R. (1998). *Professional learning communities at work: Best practices for enhancing student achievement.* Bloomington, IN: Solution Tree Press.

Earp, J. (2018). Collecting and acting on student feedback. *Teacher Magazine.* https://www.teachermagazine.com.au/articles/collecting-and-acting-on-student-feedback

Edutopia. (2016). Improving teaching with expert feedback—from students. Retrieved from https://www.edutopia.org/practice/student-surveys-using-student-voice-improve-teaching-and-learning

Farr, S. (2011). Leadership, not magic. *The Effective Educator, 68*(4), 28–33. http://www.ascd.org/publications/educational-leadership/dec10/vol68/num04/Leadership,-Not-Magic.aspx

Farr, V. (2003). The role of celebration in building classroom—learning communities. *Electronic Theses and Dissertations.* Paper 771. https://dc.etsu.edu/cgi/viewcontent.cgi?article=1928&context=etd

Fenton, B. (2019). New leaders for new schools: Forming aligned instructional leadership teams. ASCD Express. http://www.ascd.org/ascd-express/vol5/504-fenton.asp

Freire, P. (1998). Teachers as cultural workers. Letters to those who dare teach. *The edge: Critical studies in educational theory.* London, UK: Routledge.

Fullan, M. (2001). *Leading in a culture of change.* San Francisco, CA: Jossey-Bass.

Fuller, E. (2012). Examining principal turnover. *National Education Policy Center.* Retrieved from https://nepc.colorado.edu/blog/examining-principal-turnover

Gabriel, J. G. & Farmer, P. C. (2009). How to help your school thrive without breaking the bank. *ASCD.* Retrieved from http://www.ascd.org/publications/books/107042/chapters/developing-a-vision-and-a-mission.aspx

Green, T. (2015). Leading for urban school reform and community development. *University Council for Educational Administration, 51*(5), 679–711.

Gunn, J. (2018). Transformational leadership in schools [blog]. Retrieved from https://blog.sharetolearn.com/leaders-link/transformational-leadership-model/

Harrison, C., & Killion, J. (2007). Ten roles for teacher leaders. *Educational Leadership, 65*(1), 74–77. http://www.ascd.org/publications/educational-leadership/sept07/vol65/num01/Ten-Roles-for-Teacher-Leaders.aspx

Hiatt-Michael, D. B. (2001). Schools as learning communities: A vision for organic school reform [PDF]. *The School Community Journal,* 113–127. Retrieved from http://www.adi.org/journal/fw01%5CHiatt-Michael.pdf

Hogan, J. (2018). We must Maslow before we Bloom. The Compelled Educator. http://www.thecompellededucator.com/2018/03/we-must-maslow-before-we-bloom.html

Hsiao, H., & Chang, J. (2011). The role of organizational learning in transformational leadership and organizational innovation. *Asia Pacific Educational Review, 12,* 621–631.

Huffman, J., & Hipp, K. (2000). Creating communities of learners: The interaction of shared leadership, shared vision, and supportive conditions. *American Educational Research Association*, 1–18.

Huffman, J. B. & Hipp, K. K. (2012). *Reculturing schools as professional learning communities*. Lanham, MD: Scarecrow Education.

Ives, R. S. (2018). Thinking inside the box—transforming existing buildings into outstanding 21st century learning environments. Retrieved from https://spaces4learning.com/Articles/2018/05/02/Thinking-Inside-the-Box.aspx

Kageyama, N. (2019). Productive failure: A teaching method which leads to short term failure, but long term success. Bullet Proof Musician. https://bulletproofmusician.com/productive-failure-how-strategic-failure-in-the-short-term-can-lead-to-greater-success-and-learning-down-the-road/

Kark, R., Shamir, B., & Chen, G. (2003). The two faces of transformational leadership: Empowerment and dependency. *Journal of Applied Psychology, 88*(2), 246–255.

Kouzes, J., & Posner, B. (1990). *The leadership challenge: How to get extraordinary things done in organizations*. San Francisco, CA: Jossey-Bass.

Kustigian, B. M. (2013). Mission driven educational leadership—does it matter? Examining the correlations between district mission and student achievement. School Works. https://scholarworks.umass.edu/cgi/viewcontent.cgi?article=1754&context=open_access_dissertations

Johnson, J. (2015). Getting your message out (and why it's not enough). *Educational Leadership, 72*(7), 10–16. http://www.ascd.org/publications/educational-leadership/apr15/vol72/num07/Getting-Your-Message-Out-(and-Why-It's-Not-Enough).aspx

Kaffenberger, C. J. & O'Rorke-Trigiani, J. (2011). Addressing student mental health needs by providing direct and indirect services and building alliances in the community. *ASCA, 16*(5), 323–332.

Larner, M. (2004). *Pathways: Charting a course for professional learning*. Portsmouth, NH: Heinemann.

Lasic, T. (2009). Maslow before Bloom. Edu Blogs. https://human.edublogs.org/2009/08/11/maslow-before-bloom/

Leithwood, K., Jantzi, D., & Steinbeck, R. (1999). *Changing leadership for changing times*. Buckingham: Open University Press.

Leithwood, K. A., & Riehl, C. (2003). *What we know about successful school leadership*. Philadelphia, PA: Laboratory for Student Success, Temple University. http://olms.cte.jhu.edu/olms2/data/ck/file/What_we_know_about_SchoolLeadership.pdf

Lewis, D., Madison-Harris, R., Muoneke, A., & Times, C. (n.d.). Using data to guide instruction and improve student learning. *SEDL Letter, VXXII*(2). http://www.sedl.org/pubs/sedl-letter/v22n02/using-data.html

Munger, L., & von Frank, V. (2010). *Change, lead, succeed: Building capacity with school leadership teams*. Oxford, OH: NSDC. www.learningforwardstore.org

The National Education Association. (2017). Identifying stakeholders' responsibilities for closing achievement gaps: District and school based strategies. Retrieved from http://www.nea.org/home/12467.htm

Neumann, M., Jones, L., & Webb, P. (2012). Claiming the political: The forgotten terrain of teacher leadership knowledge. *Action in Teacher Education, 34*(1), 2–13.

Northhouse, P. G. (2010). *Leadership: Theory and practice*. Thousand Oaks, CA: SAGE Publications.

Office of Adolescent Health. (2016). A picture of adolescent health. https://www.hhs.gov/ash/oah/facts-and-stats/picture-of-adolescent-health/index.html

Patti, J., Holzer, A., Stern, R. S., Floman, J., & Brackett, M. A. (2018). Leading with emotional intelligence. *Educational Leadership, 75*, 46–51. http://www.ascd.org/publications/educational-leadership/summer18/vol75/num09/Leading-With-Emotional-IntelligenRonald S. Thomasce.aspx

Penuel, W. R., Riel, M., Joshi, A., Pearlman, L. Kim, C. M., & Frank, K. A. (2010). The alignment of the informal and formal organizational supports for reform: Implications for improving teaching in schools. *Education Administration Quarterly, 46*(1) 57–95.

Pepin, C. (2007). Introduction to the special issue on the media, democracy, and the politics of education. *Peabody Journal of Education, 82*(1), 1–9.

Pierson, R. (2013, May 3). *Every kid needs a champion* [Video]. TED Talk. https://www.youtube.com/watch?v=SFnMTHhKdkw

Raisman, N. (2012). Students and staff are the most important stakeholders and customers on campus [blog]. Retrieved from http://academicmaps.blogspot.com/2012/08/students-and-staff-are-most-important.html

Ravitch, D. (2000). *Left back: A century of battles over school reform.* New York, NY: Simon and Schuster.

Ross, J., & Gray, Peter. (2006). School leadership and student achievement: The mediating effects of teacher beliefs. *Canadian Journal of Education, 26*(3), 798–822.

Senge, P. (2012). Creating the schools of the future: Education for a sustainable society. *The Solutions Journal, 3*(3), 115–118. Retrieved from https://www.thesolutionsjournal.com/article/creating-the-schools-of-the-future-education-for-a-sustainable-society/

Shafer, L. (2017). Making student feedback work: New advice on building a culture of feedback and making it meaningful for teachers. https://www.gse.harvard.edu/news/uk/17/11/making-student-feedback-work

Sheldon, S., & Epstein, J. L. (2002). Improving student behavior and school discipline with family and community involvement. *Education and Urban Society, 35*(1), 4–26.

Sheppard, B., & Brown, J. (2009). Developing and implementing a shared vision of teaching and learning at the district level. *International Studies in Educational Administration, 37*(2), 41–59.

Smith, K. (2014). Disaggregation of data in a RtI/PBIS framework [PDF]. *Wisconsin RtI Center/Wisconsin PBIS Network.*

Tassione, G., & Inlay, L. (2014). Inside out: The power of relationships. *Educational Leadership, 72*(1). http://www.ascd.org/publications/educational-leadership/sept14/vol72/num01/Inside-Out@-The-Power-of-Relationships.aspx

The U.S. Department of Health and Human Services. (2019). A picture of adolescent health. Retrieved from https://www.hhs.gov/ash/oah/facts-and-stats/picture-of-adolescent-health/index.html

Thiers, N. (2018). On the front lines of mental health. *Mental Health in Schools, 75*(1), 7–7. http://www.ascd.org/publications/educational-leadership/dec17/vol75/num04/On-the-Front-Lines-of-Mental-Health.aspx

Thomas, R. S. (2011). My nine 'truths' of data analysis. *Education Week.* https://www.edweek.org/ew/articles/2011/06/15/35thomas.h30.html

Trumbull, E., & Rothstein-Fisch, C. (2008). *Managing diverse classrooms: How to build on students' cultural strengths.* Alexandria, VA: ASCD.

Yang, Y. (2013). Principals' transformational leadership in school improvement. *Journal of Academic Administration in Higher Education, 9*(2), 77–83. https://files.eric.ed.gov/fulltext/EJ1140974.pdf

INDEX

A

abandoning top-down approach, 34–35
Academically Intellectually Gifted (AIG), 3
Allison, D. J., 54
American College Testing (ACT), 6
Anderson, A, 8
Argyris, C., 56
Arter, J. A., 14
assessment *See* needs assessment
"Assessment for Learning", 14
attitude of excellence, 53–55
Austin, S., 95
automatic communication, 107
autonomous communication, 107

B

Bagshaw, M., 55
Bear, G. G., 16
Beatty, B., 124–125
behavior(s), 15–16
behavioral communication, 15–16
behavioral data, 14–15 27
Bloom Versus Maslow, 80–81
Brackett, M. A., 125
Bragg, S., 44–45
Brown, J., 37
Buchanan, R., 37
Burkhauser, S., 24

C

Campbell, P., 76
capital *See* social capital
career and technical education (CTE), 6
Carver, C. W., 63
celebration, questions, 71–72
challenges, school, 7–9 78–86
champion, 62–63
change, 132–137
    community stakeholders, 137
    individual teacher leaders, 136–137
    instructional lead team (ILT), 134–136
    overview, 132–134
    parents/guardians, 137
    school improvement team (SIT), 134–136
change agents *See* students as change agents
Comer, J., 63
communication, 99–107
    automatic, 107
    autonomous, 107
    behavioral, 15–16
    with teacher leaders, 99–107
community stakeholders, 137 144
Compton, B, 34
content area data, 14 27–28
Courville, K., 118
Covey, S. R., 39
culture of high expectations, 55–56

D

data
    analyzing, 124 126–131
    behavioral, 14–15 27
    collection, 112–121
    content area, 14 27–28
    disaggregating, 126–131
    emotion, 124–126
    formal, 12–13 26
    implementation guide, 127–131
    informal, 12–13 26
    overview, 122–124
    physical, 17–18 28–29
Deal, T., 37
Delisio, E. R., 28
Democracy and Education (Dewey), 40
Denmark, V., 142
Dewey, J., 40 45
"Disaggregation of Data in a RtI/PBIS Framework", 16
DuFour, R., 38

E

Eaker, R., 38
Earp, J., 47–48
"Easy Ways to Market Your Schools" (Delisio), 28
education *See* public education
Education Value-Added Assessment System (EVAAS), 3
Elementary and Secondary Education Act (1965), 35
emotion, 124–126
end-of-grade (EOG) scores, 3 12 43 70 99–100 132 134
English language arts (ELA), 7 12 48 79 100 123 133–134
Epstein, J. L., 137
ethnocentrism, 55

evaluators *See* students as evaluators
Every Kid Needs a Champion, 63
Every Student Succeeds Act, 35

F
Facebook, 42
facility walk-through, 19–20
failure *See* productive failure
Fannie Tyson (FT) Elementary, 3–9 69
    change, 132–134
    instructional lead team, 90–91
    mission statement, 22–23
    mobile office, 109–110
    needs assessment, 11 14–15 17–18
    students as change agents, 50–51
    students as evaluators, 42–44
    students as stakeholders, 34–35
    transformation and testing, 139–140
Farmer, P. C., 26–27
Farr, S., 71
feedback, 44–45
Fenton, B., 94
Fielding, M., 44–45
"First-Year Principals in Urban School Districts", 24–25
formal data, 12–13 26
Fortune 500, 45
Freire, P., 46
Fullan, M., 118
Fuller, E., 24

G
Gabriel, J. G., 26–27
Google Hangout, 39
Green, T., 137
guardians, 137
Gunn, J., 134 136

H
Harrison, C., 107
health *See* socioemotional health
hearing ears, 85–86
Hiatt-Michael, D. B., 38
Hipp, K., 35 38
Hogan, J., 86
Huffman, J., 35 38

I
"Identifying Stakeholders' Responsibilities for Closing Achievement Gaps: Stakeholder Actions", 37
"Improving Teaching With Expert Feedback—From Students", 48
informal data, 12–13 26
Inlay, L., 67
instructional lead team (ILT), 70 76 79 90–97
    change, 134–136
    local instructional programming, 123
    mission statement, 23 92–93

    mobile office, 112
    needs assessment, 12 17 126
    overview, 90–92
    pragmatic, 93–95
    productive failure, 143
    scheduling school leader, 95–97
    school, 6–7
    school leaders, 130
    students as change agents, 50–51 53
    students as evaluators, 43 46–48
    transformation and testing, 140
Ives, R. S., 19

J
Jantzi, D., 36
Johnson, J., 102–103
Jones, L., 4

K
Kaffenberger, C. J., 17
Kageyama, N., 143–144
Killion, J., 107
Kustigian, B. M., 93

L
Lasic, T., 80–81
leaders *See* teacher leaders
leadership
    defined, 40
    gap, 52–53
    teacher, 4
    transformational, 36 52
learning
    communities, 38 112
    environment, 61
    student-centered, 53
Leithwood, K., 36 52–54
Lewis, D., 126
location, 16–17

M
major behaviors, 15–16
Managing Diverse Classrooms: How to Build on Students' Cultural Strengths (Trumbull), 72
marketing, mission statement, 28–29
memo, 103–106
mental health, 17 27
minor behaviors, 15–16
mission statement, 22–29
    defined, 26
    developing, 25–28
    instructional lead team (ILT), 92–93
    marketing, 28–29
    overview, 22–24
    reciting, 24–25
mobile office, 109–122
    basics, 111
    data collection, 112
    instructional lead team (ILT), 112

overview, 109–111
questions, 111–112
technology, 118
Munger, L., 135

N

National Education Association, 37
needs assessment, 11–20
  behavioral communication, 15–16
  behavioral data, 14–15 27
  content area data, 14 27–28
  facility walk-through, 19–20
  Fannie Tyson (FT) Elementary, 11 14–15 17–18
  formal data, 12–13 26
  informal data, 12–13 26
  instructional lead team (ILT), 12 16 126
  location, 16–17
  mental health, 17 27
  overview, 11–12
  physical data, 17–18 28–29
  school improvement team (SIT), 19–20
  shifting perspective, 18–19
  3-year trends, 13 26
Neumann, M., 4
No Child Left Behind, 35

O

Office of Adolescent Health, 62
One-Minute Meeting
  conceptual framework, 36–38 38
  data analysis implementation guide, 127–131
  data collection template, 113–121
  implementation, 64–66 72–75 82–84 104–105 112
  mobile office, 111–112
  process, 29 36–37 38 42 44 49 52–53 55–56 67 71–72 79 81 90 94–95 103 107 110 118 125 132 134 136 139 142
  sample, 105–106
  school as learning communities, 38
  shared vision, 37
  strategy, 54
  student stakeholders, 36–37
  success, 109
  transformational leadership, 36
opportunities for feedback, 44–45
organizational vision, 20

P

parents, 33 137
Parent-Teacher Organization, 35
Patti, J., 125
Penuel, W. R., 13
Pepin, C., 48
perspective, 18–19
Peterson, K., 37
physical data, 17–18 28–29
Picture of Adolescent Health, 62–63
Pierson, R. F., 62–63

Positive Behavior Interventions & Supports (PBIS) program, 3
power *See* sharing power
pragmatic, ILT, 93–95
productive failure, 143–145
professional learning community (PLC), 29 70 79 85 91 94 132 136
public education, 34
public schools, 8–9 *See also* school
Public Schools and Weberian Bureaucracy: A Summary (Allison), 54

Q

questions, 60–67
  Bloom Versus Maslow, 80–81
  celebration, 71–72
  champion, 62–63
  hearing ears, 85–86
  icebreaker, 66–67
  implementing, 64–66 72–75 81–84
  mobile office, 111–112
  option, 76
  overview, 60–62 69–71 78–80
  walking feet, 85–86

R

Raisman, N., 4
Ravitch, D., 92–93
reciting, mission statement, 24–25
report cards, school, 6–7
Riehl, C., 52–54

S

scheduling school leader, 95–97
Schón, D., 56
school, 2–9
  accountability, 7
  challenges, 7–9 78–86
  improvement, 101–103 142
  leader, 95–97
  as learning communities, 38
  overview, 2–4
  report cards, 6–7
  transformation, 4–6
school improvement team (SIT), 94 96 102 118 123 125–126 130
  change, 134–136
  mission statement, 22–23 29
  needs assessment, 19–20
  productive failure, 143
  students as change agents, 50 52–53
  students as evaluators, 43 47–48
"Schools as Learning Communities: A Vision for Organic School Reform" (Hiatt-Michael), 38
Senge, P., 34–35 37
Shafer, L., 44 46
shared vision, 37
sharing power, 142
Sheldon, S., 137

Sheppard, B., 37
shifting perspective, 18–19
Skype, 39
Smith, K., 16
social capital, 52–54
social media, 29
socioemotional health, 17
stakeholders *See* students as stakeholders
21st century, students, 39–40
Steinbeck, R., 36
student(s)
    achievement, 7 13–14 35 51 93 143
    celebration, 71–72
    feedback, 44
    surveys, 47–49
    teaching evaluative language, 45–47
student-centered learning, 53
students as change agents, 50–56
    addressing the leadership gap, 52–53
    attitude of excellence, 53–55
    culture of high expectations, 55–56
    overview, 50–52
    school improvement team (SIT), 50 52–53
students as evaluators, 42–49
    instructional lead team (ILT), 43 46–48
    opportunities for feedback, 44–45
    overview, 42–44
    school improvement team (SIT), 42 47–48
    student surveys, 47–49
    teaching evaluative language, 45–47
students as stakeholders, 32–40
    21st century, 39–40
    abandoning top-down approach, 34–35
    one-minute meeting conceptual framework, 36–38
    overview, 32–34

T
Tassione, G., 67
teacher leaders, 99–107
    automatic to autonomy, 106–107

memo, 103–106
overview, 99–101
school improvement, 101–103
teacher leadership, 4
Teachers as Cultural Workers: Letters to Those Who Dare Teach (Freire), 46
teaching evaluative language, 45–47
technology, 118
"Thinking Inside the Box", 19
Thomas, R. S., 130
three-year trends, 13 26
top-down approach, 34–35
transformation
    leadership, 36 52
    overview, 139–142
    people, 145–146
    process, 142–143
    productive failure, 143–145
    school, 4–6
    testing and, 139–146
Trumbull, E., 72

U
U.S. Department of Health and Human Services, 62

V
von Frank, V., 135

W
walking feet, 85–86
Walmart© Conversation, 7–9 42 139
Webb, P., 4
World Wide Web, 62

Y
Yang, Y., 142–143

CPSIA information can be obtained
at www.ICGtesting.com
Printed in the USA
BVHW052316040122
625511BV00001B/4